United States Presidents

Franklin D. Roosevelt

Series Consultant:
Don M. Coerver, professor of history
Texas Christian University, Fort Worth, Texas

Karen Bornemann Spies

Enslow Publishers, Inc.

40 Industrial Road   PO Box 38
Box 398   Aldershot
Berkeley Heights, NJ 07922   Hants GU12 6BP
USA   UK

http://www.enslow.com

Copyright © 1999 by Karen Bornemann Spies

Library of Congress Cataloging-in-Publication Data

Spies, Karen Bornemann.
    Franklin D. Roosevelt / Karen B. Spies
      p. cm. — (United States presidents)
    Includes bibliographical references and index.
    Summary: A biography of the thirty-second president of the United
States, the only man to be elected president four times.
    ISBN 0-7660-1038-4
    1. Roosevelt, Franklin D. (Franklin Delano), 1882–1945—Juvenile
literature. 2. Presidents—United States—Biography—Juvenile
literature. [1. Roosevelt, Franklin D. (Franklin Delano),
1882–1945. 2. Presidents.] I. Title. II. Series.
E807.S65   1999
973.917'092—dc21
[b]   98-19645
                                      CIP
                                      AC

Printed in the United States of America

10 9 8 7 6 5 4 3

Illustration Credits: Franklin D. Roosevelt Library, pp. 4, 11, 13,
19, 22, 25, 28, 33, 37, 46, 57, 69, 87, 102, 104; Karen Bornemann
Spies, p. 111; Library of Congress, pp. 43, 71; National Archives,
p. 103; U.S. Naval Historical Center, p. 90.

Source Document Credits: Captain Glenn Howell, 1974, U.S.
Naval Historical Center, p. 93; Franklin D. Roosevelt Library, pp. 15,
36, 91; Library of Congress, pp. 62, 72, 75, 79; National Archives,
p. 96; U.S. Naval Historical Center, p. 89.

Cover Illustration: Franklin D. Roosevelt Library.

Contents

In his third term as president, on December 8, 1941, the day after the Japanese attacked Pearl Harbor, Roosevelt signed a declaration of war against Japan.

1

TRIAL by FIRE

In the summer of 1920, after having held several important government positions, Franklin Delano Roosevelt was nominated by the Democratic party for vice-president of the United States. The Democratic candidate for president was Governor James M. Cox of Ohio. That fall, they lost the election. Roosevelt was thirty-eight years old.

By 1921, Roosevelt was back working in private business, although surely he was planning to run again for public office. He was ready for a much needed vacation.

His wife, Eleanor, and their five children were already at the family vacation cottage on Campobello Island, located in Canadian waters off the coast of Maine. Roosevelt sailed to Campobello aboard a friend's yacht at the beginning of August. The captain was not familiar with the coastal waters, so Roosevelt took the wheel much of the voyage. Rough seas made the trip difficult, so he was very tired when they arrived at Campobello. Nevertheless, he took the yacht's owner and other friends out fishing. At one point, Roosevelt fell overboard. He later wrote, ". . . the water was so cold it seemed paralyzing."[1]

On Wednesday, August 10, the Roosevelts went sailing on the family's yacht, the *Vireo*. They spotted a forest fire on a nearby island and beat out the flames with pine branches. Sooty and dirty, they sailed back to Campobello. After a quick swim in a warm lagoon, they jogged two miles across the island. Roosevelt then swam in the icy waters of the Bay of Fundy. He later commented, "I didn't feel the usual reaction, the glow I'd expected."[2] When he returned to the house, Roosevelt sat on the porch in his wet swimsuit and read the day's newspapers and mail. Too tired to change clothes for dinner, he went upstairs to bed. He would never walk on his own again.

By the end of the next day, his legs were paralyzed and his temperature reached 102 degrees. The local doctor, E. H. Bennett, diagnosed a heavy cold. But Roosevelt's condition worsened. By August 12, he was paralyzed from the waist down. The next day, Dr. Bennett decided that his diagnosis had been wrong. Another physician, Dr. William W. Keen, was vacationing nearby. Dr. Keen felt that a blood clot had

The Roosevelt family vacation retreat on Campobello Island located off the coast of Maine in Canadian waters.

settled in Roosevelt's lower back. The clot prevented Roosevelt from moving, but not from experiencing pain. Keen prescribed deep massage to help dissolve the clot. But the massages only caused agonizing pain.

In desperation, Eleanor Roosevelt consulted a specialist from Boston, Massachusetts, Dr. Robert W. Lovett. On August 25, Dr. Lovett immediately diagnosed poliomyelitis, or polio. The dreaded disease was often called infantile paralysis, because it usually attacked children. It sometimes paralyzed the entire body or even caused death. At that time, doctors did not understand its cause or why some cases were more severe than others. Today the vaccine developed in 1955 by Jonas Salk protects us from polio.

Since he had spent little time with other children when he was growing up, Roosevelt had been exposed to very few childhood illnesses. Experts now believe he suffered a particularly intense case of polio because his immunity to disease was low. In addition, he was tired from overwork. Such stress further lowered his resistance to disease.[3]

Dr. Lovett ordered the massages stopped because they were damaging fragile muscles. He prescribed hot baths to make Roosevelt feel more comfortable. He suggested rest and simple exercises. The planned summer vacation became what Eleanor Roosevelt later called a "trial by fire."[4]

At first, his children would not come past the sickroom door. Roosevelt reassured the youngsters with his determined cheerfulness. To involve them in his therapy, he pulled back his bed covers and showed them his withered legs. He explained the names of the muscles and how they worked. They cheered when he reported progress with his exercises.[5]

However, Franklin D. Roosevelt would never again walk without crutches. Fighting the effects of polio would build Roosevelt's powers of perseverance in everything he did. This perseverance eventually allowed him to go on to a brilliant political career.

He was elected governor of New York for the first of

two terms in 1928. In 1932, he became president of the United States. He became chief executive at a time when the United States faced its greatest crises since the Civil War.

Roosevelt reacted with optimism and confidence to lead the United States through the Great Depression, a severe downturn in the nation's economic well-being, and through World War II. He was the only elected leader in history who could not walk on his own.[6] His bout with polio had clearly hastened his transformation from a somewhat spoiled, superficial young man to a tough and determined leader.

2

A PRIVILEGED BIRTH

Franklin Delano Roosevelt was born into a privileged family with deep roots in our nation's past. The first Roosevelts came to America from Holland in about 1650. The ancestors on his mother's side, the Delanos, settled in Plymouth Colony in 1621. Franklin's mother, Sara Delano Roosevelt, was known in New York society as one of "the beautiful Delano sisters."[1] Even as a young woman, Sara had a regal manner. She shocked her family when she married fifty-two-year-old James Roosevelt, a widower who lived near the Delano estate on the Hudson River. Twenty-six-year-old Sara was the same age as James's son from his first marriage. But Sara found in James someone who shared her beliefs about education and behavior.

Two years after the marriage, on January 30, 1882,

Franklin was born. His birth was so difficult that both mother and child nearly died. Franklin was blue and limp, but artificial respiration helped him start breathing. His proud father wrote in his diary that Franklin "weighed 10 lbs. without clothes."[2]

James Roosevelt earned most of his money from investments in coal and railroads. Business sometimes

Franklin was about one-and-a-half years old when this photograph was taken of him sitting on his father's shoulder.

brought James to New York City or Washington, D.C. The Roosevelts spent the winter of 1887 in the capital. James had contributed to President Grover Cleveland's election campaign. The elder Roosevelt took his five-year-old son to visit the president. Cleveland put his hand on Franklin's head. "My little man," he said. "I am making a strange wish for you. It is that you may never be President of the United States."[3] President Cleveland's wish paralleled the hopes of Franklin's parents. They wanted nothing more for their son than the continuation of the comfortable life they lived.

James's investments allowed him to spend the bulk of his time at Springwood, the Roosevelt estate. Springwood extended over nine hundred acres of woods and farmlands just south of the village of Hyde Park, New York. Each day, James toured the fields and barns of his estate. Beginning at age four, Franklin, mounted on his own pony, accompanied his father on these tours. He not only learned about the operations of the estate, but also built a close relationship with his father. Franklin nicknamed him Popsy, indicating the depth of their bond.

The elder Roosevelt was old enough to be Franklin's grandfather. But he played an active role in his son's upbringing. James took his son sledding before Franklin was two years old. On one occasion, Sara wrote in her diary that "dear James strained his knee" while tobogganing with Franklin.[4] James also spent many afternoons sailing and fishing with his son.

Franklin was the focus of his mother's attention from the moment he was born. Although she had servants and a nursemaid, Sara bathed her baby herself and nursed him until he was almost one year old. She kept Franklin in long dresses and his hair in ringlets until he was nearly six. This style of grooming was customary for the wealthy social classes in those days. He was not allowed to take a bath alone until he was eight years old. Each day, Sara read aloud to him. She encouraged him in his hobbies, including one that she had always

In 1885, Franklin posed on a donkey with his dog Budgy at the Roosevelt estate called Springwood, just south of Hyde Park, New York.

been interested in—stamp collecting. Sara kept a diary of her son's activities until he was in his twenties.

When Franklin was grown, Sara insisted that she had never "tried to influence him against his own tastes . . . or shape his life."[5] But she was strong-willed enough to believe that whatever she wished for her son was in his best interests. Franklin soon learned that the best way to get along with his mother was to seem to agree with her. He used charm and a warm smile to get his way. He sometimes skipped church by pleading a headache, which would miraculously be gone by afternoon. His parents called them his "Sunday headaches."[6] If he wanted to avoid practicing for his piano lesson, he complained that he had "a bobo," or scratch on his finger.[7] As an adult, Franklin demonstrated similar charm. Aides and voters came away from meetings certain that he had agreed with their viewpoints, which was not always the case.

As a child, Franklin seemed happy and secure. But he was totally unaware that not everyone lived such a luxurious life. His mother felt he was "a good little boy" who chose the right behavior "instinctively."[8] Always doing the right thing must have been tiresome. One day Franklin told his mother that he wanted more freedom.[9] She and James agreed that perhaps they had restricted their son too much. Franklin spent the next day doing whatever he wanted. However, according to his mother, on the following morning, he resumed his original routine.[10]

SOURCE DOCUMENT

For MAMA 1889
FROM
FRANKLIN

MY DEAR MAMA. I WILL TELL
YOU WHAT I WANT FOR CHRIST=
MAS. I WANT A BOX OF BLOCKS
AND A TRAIN OF CARS AND SOME
LITTLE BOATS BUT I THINK I
DON'T WANT ANYTHING ELSE
GOOD-BYE YOUR LOVING

FRANKLIN

When Franklin was seven, he wrote this note to his mother asking for certain Christmas gifts. The birds and hat at the top were already printed on the notepaper.

Nevertheless, Franklin showed occasional signs of spunk. Until he was about four years old, he had temper tantrums whenever he lost at games with his mother. At age nine, Franklin climbed one of the giant oak trees at Springwood and remained there until darkness fell. He enjoyed watching the frantic servants and his worried mother looking for him.

Growing up, Franklin spent more time with adults than with other children. Almost everyone he associated with came from a small circle of wealthy families. Archie Rogers, Jr., and his younger brother, Edmund, lived nearby. Archie became Franklin's best friend. In 1889, when Franklin was seven, Archie died of diphtheria. Archie's death must have deeply affected Franklin. However, Sara did not write about the death or Franklin's reactions to it in her diary. Such a lack of emotional response was typical of Sara's belief that grief must be kept to oneself.[11] She raised her son to act in a similar manner. As an adult, Franklin faced his public and private challenges by trying not to show any feelings of sadness or anger.

Franklin's friendships were strictly controlled by Sara. No children spent the night. Sometimes Franklin was allowed to play outside the house with children of Springwood employees. But these children recognized that Franklin held a position of authority. One winter day, two farmer's sons were allowed to sled with Franklin. However, they, not he, always had to pull the sled back uphill.

Franklin's mother taught him beginning reading and writing. After he was six years old, he studied under several governesses and tutors. They taught him subjects such as German, French, history, geography, science, and arithmetic. The governess who influenced him the most was Mademoiselle Jeanne Sandoz. She taught all Franklin's subjects in French with the exception of English and German. Mlle. Sandoz was convinced that Franklin would go far.

Franklin followed a rigid daily schedule. He had to get up at 7:00 A.M. Breakfast was served an hour later. From 9:00 until noon, he had lessons, followed by playtime and lunch. Franklin then had additional lessons until 4:00 P.M. Next came free time, which he spent outdoors or pursuing his hobbies. At 6:00 P.M., he ate supper and then went to bed two hours later.

Franklin's parents felt that travel overseas would give him a broader view of the world. Before he was fifteen years old, Franklin had made eight trips to Europe, beginning at age three. The family sailed on deluxe ocean liners. Their fellow travelers were members of high society or royalty.

To travel by land in the United States, the Roosevelts used a private railroad car, the *Monon*. Its elegant bedrooms and sitting rooms were decorated in brass and mahogany. Franklin soon developed a love of trains, which remained his preferred manner of cross-country travel as an adult.

James Roosevelt passed on his love of animals to his

son. Franklin was not quite seven when he received a Welsh pony named Debby. Franklin's father expected him to feed and groom her. He felt that his young son was capable of handling such responsibility.[12] Franklin was also given a series of dogs and was expected to take care of them as well. His red setter, Marksman, went along whenever Franklin rode or hiked at the Springwood estate.

Franklin's love of the Springwood grounds developed into a lifelong interest in the outdoors and in conservation. He collected birds' nests and eggs. When Franklin wanted to expand his collection to include birds, James gave him a shotgun for his eleventh birthday. He was allowed to use it on the condition that he shoot only one bird of each species. By the time he was fourteen, he had shot and identified more than three hundred types of birds. At first, Franklin's mother opposed his use of a gun. But Sara was soon proud of his skills and displayed the bird specimens on shelves and in cases.

Working on his collections offered Franklin a sense of independence and times of peaceful solitude.[13] It also allowed him the chance to put order into his own world, instead of having adults, especially his mother, structure all of it for him.

Franklin's interest in the sea developed from listening to his Grandfather Delano and his mother tell exciting seafaring stories. His grandfather's collection of ship models under glass inspired Franklin to carve and

Franklin was eleven years old when he posed for this formal photograph with his strong-willed mother, Sara Delano Roosevelt.

collect his own miniature ships. In the attic of the Delano home, Franklin found whalers' logs, large books bound in canvas. These old naval reports, with whales stenciled in the margins, stirred Franklin's imagination. By age fourteen, Franklin had read Alfred T. Mahan's *The Influence of Sea Power Upon History*. This work stressed the importance of a large navy and later influenced Franklin's decisions after he became assistant secretary of the Navy in 1913.

His interest in the sea caused what may have been the only time Franklin risked a strong argument with his father.[14] He deeply wanted to attend the United States Naval Academy in Annapolis, Maryland. But his father felt it would be cruel for an only son to be away from his parents for as much time as a naval career demanded. Franklin never got over this refusal and maintained a love of the Navy his entire life.

Summers at Campobello developed Franklin's seafaring skills. In 1891, James purchased a fifty-one-foot yacht, the *Half Moon*, and taught nine-year-old Franklin how to sail. When he was sixteen, Franklin received his own twenty-one-foot knockabout, or small sailboat, the *New Moon*. It had a cozy cabin with two bunks. He was soon skilled in navigating the treacherous tides and currents of the rocky Maine coastline and the Bay of Fundy.

In the autumn of 1896, Franklin's life changed dramatically. He enrolled at Groton School, a college-preparatory school for boys in Massachusetts. Most of its students came from families of high society. The majority of boys started at Groton when they were twelve years old. But Franklin's mother had kept him at home until he was fourteen, which put him at a disadvantage. He was the new boy in a group that had already formed tight friendships. Later, as an adult, Franklin told a friend, "I always felt entirely out of things" at Groton.[15]

Franklin wanted badly to fit in. He tried out for several sports, because Groton's leading students were top athletes. Unfortunately, he weighed only one hundred pounds. Franklin was too small to be a success. He played on the Bum Baseball Boys, a team made up of the worst players, and on the seventh-best out of eight football teams. He earned his only athletic ribbon as manager of the baseball team during his last year at Groton.

However, Franklin made his mark in an unusual sport known as the high kick. It was done only at Groton. The athlete leaped high in the air and kicked at a tin pan hanging from the gymnasium ceiling. Franklin succeeded because he kept practicing until he was black and blue. He reached a height of seven feet, three and a half inches, which was two feet higher than he stood.

Franklin's letters home from Groton revealed little of his pain in adjusting. Instead, he wrote what he knew his mother wanted to hear. That first September, Franklin noted that he was getting along well with his classmates.[16] But this was not quite true. As a result of

In October 1899, Franklin was a member of the second football team at Groton School. He is second from the left in the front row, wearing a white sweater.

his frequent travels abroad, he spoke with an accent. The other boys thought it sounded phony.

The headmaster at Groton, Reverend Endicott Peabody, made a lasting impression on Franklin. Franklin may even have thought of Peabody as a substitute for his father, who by then was in his seventies and in poor health. Peabody's strong sense of right and wrong shaped Franklin's ideals. Peabody believed that the wealth and privileged upbringing of his students obligated them to help others. He said, "If some Groton boys do not enter political life and do something for our land, it won't be because they have not been urged."[17]

Peabody modeled Groton after a typical English boarding school. Franklin, like the other students, lived in a six-by-nine-foot room. Instead of a door, it had a curtain. The rector felt that too much privacy harmed the morals of adolescent boys. But Franklin loved his tiny cubicle, because it was his own.

During his first year, Franklin studied Latin, Greek, algebra, English literature and composition, French, ancient history, science, and the Bible. He was not an outstanding scholar. He earned Cs and Bs. However, he achieved a near-perfect score for neatness and a perfect rating for punctuality. Ironically, his classmates looked down on perfect behavior. So Franklin decided to try to get in trouble. Finally, after eight months in school, he achieved a black mark against him for talking in class. He wrote to his mother about how proud he was finally to have a demerit, since this proved to the other boys that he did have some school spirit after all.[18]

In the spring of 1897, Franklin was thrilled to have his fifth cousin, Theodore "Teddy" Roosevelt, visit Groton. Teddy had just been appointed assistant secretary of the Navy. He gave an exciting talk about his experiences when he was on the Police Board for New York City. His appearance at the school brought prestige to Franklin.

In late April 1898, the Spanish-American War broke out. Franklin and two of his friends planned to run away from school and enlist in the U.S. Navy. Their idea was unrealistic, because the boys were too young to serve in the military anyway. However, Franklin came down with scarlet fever, which ruined their plans. His parents returned from Europe to check on his health. Franklin lay in an isolation ward at Groton. But that did not stop his mother from visiting him. Sara placed a stepladder outside her son's second-floor window. She climbed it each day and talked and read to him through the open window.

During Franklin's remaining career at Groton, he joined the debate team, performed in the school play, and worked on the newspaper. When Franklin's vision worsened, he chose gold pince-nez eyeglasses with no earpieces. They were like those of his cousin, Theodore Roosevelt, who was by then governor of New York.

Franklin graduated from Groton in the upper quarter of his class of nineteen. He won a forty-volume set of Shakespeare's works for writing the best essay in Latin. Reverend Peabody wrote years later that Franklin had been a "quiet, satisfactory boy," with excellent intelligence, but not brilliant.[19] Little of the Groton curriculum prepared Franklin Roosevelt for political leadership, despite Reverend Peabody's goals. The history courses covered ancient and European but not American history.

Some historians trace Roosevelt's concern for the underprivileged to his training at Groton.[20] Franklin joined the Missionary Society and in 1900, served as

Franklin served as the manager of the baseball team during his last year at Groton, his college preparatory school. He is standing in the middle of the back row.

director of its summer camp for poor boys. In addition, twice weekly he visited an eighty-four-year-old widow. He and a classmate made sure she was never without coal, water, and food.

In September 1900, Franklin entered Harvard University in Cambridge, Massachusetts. He had grown tall and handsome, with a ready smile, perfected with the help of orthodontic braces. Lathrop Brown, a friend from Groton, was his roommate. They lived in an apartment in Westmorly Court, an exclusive dormitory in the wealthy Gold Coast area of Cambridge.

Outside the classroom, he became involved in politics for the first time. The Republicans chose Theodore Roosevelt as their vice-presidential candidate in 1900. Franklin joined the Harvard Republican Club and enthusiastically campaigned for his cousin.

Early in his freshman year, on December 8, 1900, Franklin's father died, after many years of heart trouble. That Christmas was an especially sad one for both Franklin and his mother. Sara was only forty-six years old and desperately missed her husband. After her first winter as a widow, she rented an apartment in Boston so that she could be nearer to her son. This move severely challenged his independence.

As he had done at Groton, Franklin tried hard to fit in at Harvard. To achieve notice at Harvard, a student had to excel in sports, outside activities, or academics. But Franklin was still considered too small for most sports. Although he had grown seven inches taller, he weighed only 145 pounds. He was too light for the freshman football or rowing teams.

Franklin suffered a crushing disappointment when he failed to gain acceptance to an elite social club. The clubs controlled campus social life. In the fall of Franklin's sophomore year, the clubs began to select members. Franklin was invited to join Delta Kappa Epsilon, known as "the Dickey." From this group, members of the Porcellian, the most elite club, were selected. His cousin Theodore Roosevelt and his father had both been members. As a legacy, or close relative of former members, Franklin expected to make the Porcellian, but he did not. He never learned the reason he was denied membership, but he never got over the rejection. Fifteen years later, he referred to it as "the greatest disappointment of his life."[21] However, his future wife, Eleanor, felt the disappointment made him more sympathetic to those who had been left out.[22]

Franklin was highly successful in his work on the Harvard *Crimson*, the school newspaper. In his third year, he earned the top position of president for the first semester of the following year. The president served as editor-in-chief, who wrote all the editorials and chose the articles to be published. Franklin's connections with Theodore Roosevelt helped. Teddy visited Boston when he was vice-president. Franklin called him and learned that his cousin was going to lecture in a Harvard course the next morning. Franklin won a scoop—or the publishing of a piece of news before any rival publication—for the *Crimson* by reporting this news. Two thousand students and spectators showed up for the lecture. Although the scoop helped Franklin earn his editorship, the main reason for his success was his continued hard work.

Franklin was not an outstanding student, earning a "gentleman C" average.[23] He majored in history and government. However, he finished his degree in three years because he had taken advanced placement courses at Groton. He stayed on at Harvard for another year to serve as president of the newspaper. His editorials showed no signs of his future political leanings or

Roosevelt (center of front row) served as president and editor-in-chief of the Harvard Crimson, *the school newspaper, during his fourth year at the university.*

brilliance. They covered mundane issues such as the lack of spirit at football games and the need for more campus sidewalks.

He also took graduate-level courses in economics and history. His courses seemed as if they might adequately prepare him to be a future statesman, but, in fact, they covered little of the real workings of government. Franklin said his classes were "like an electric lamp that hasn't any wire. You need the lamp for light but it's useless if you can't switch it on."[24]

In 1904, he was elected to a class office. This budding interest in the world of politics would ultimately bring him fame.

3

ANNA ELEANOR

One of the most important decisions Franklin D. Roosevelt made at Harvard was to marry Anna Eleanor Roosevelt. Franklin and Eleanor, as she called herself, were distant cousins. They were descended from two brothers, Johannes and Jacobus Roosevelt. Franklin was the great-great-great grandson of Jacobus. Eleanor was the great-great-great-great granddaughter of Johannes.

Franklin and Eleanor had known each other all their lives. However, although they were related, they came from very different backgrounds. Franklin had a secure, loving childhood and demonstrated an air of self-confidence. Eleanor's childhood was hard. Her handsome father, Elliott, was Theodore Roosevelt's younger brother. Elliott Roosevelt showed great charm but none of his brother's drive to succeed. Elliott became an alcoholic who spent much time away from his family seeking treatment. Eleanor's mother, society beauty Anna Hall Roosevelt, seemed embarrassed by her daughter's serious personality and plain appearance. She made fun of Eleanor by calling her "Granny," which seriously questioned Eleanor's self-confidence.[1] Eleanor's mother died when Eleanor was eight. Then her father died when she was ten. She and her two brothers were forced to go live with their harsh, unloving Grandmother Mary Hall.

When she was fifteen, Eleanor's life changed dramatically. In September 1899, she was sent to Allenswood, a finishing school in England, where she developed poise and self-confidence. Eleanor earned admiration for her intelligence and her loyal friendships. She called her three years at Allenswood, "the happiest years of my life."[2]

Eleanor had to leave Allenswood because Grandmother Hall wanted her to make her debut. Debuts, or "coming out" balls, were where debutantes, wealthy young women from selected families, were presented to society. On her way home from Allenswood in 1902, Eleanor took a train from New York City to her grandmother's estate on the Hudson River. Franklin and his mother happened to be on the same train. Eleanor impressed her cousin with her interesting conversation. For the first time, he began to view Eleanor as an appealing young woman.

They began to see more of each other at the debutante events. Few people, including Sara Roosevelt, realized that they were falling in love. Even Eleanor had trouble believing that charming, handsome Franklin would be interested in her.[3]

Eleanor's serious side attracted Franklin. She worked at a New York City settlement house, a place that provided help for the poor. Eleanor taught exercise and dance classes to underprivileged children, an unusual activity for an upper-class young woman.

Franklin was also interested in Eleanor because she was Theodore Roosevelt's favorite niece. Her uncle had assumed the presidency after President McKinley's death in 1901. An opportunity to strengthen his ties with her uncle would be useful to Franklin's political career.

On June 24, 1903, Franklin graduated from Harvard. After a summer trip to Europe, he returned to Harvard for his fourth year to work on the *Crimson*. That fall, Franklin asked Eleanor to marry him. The proposed marriage came as a complete surprise to Sara Roosevelt. It was a clear indication that Franklin wanted more independence from her. She told the couple that she felt they were too young to be married and asked them to keep the engagement secret for a year.

In the meantime, she hoped Franklin would lose interest in marriage. She took him on a five-week Caribbean cruise, hoping to distract him. But Franklin returned even more eager to spend time with Eleanor.

Finally, Sara accepted Franklin's determination to marry Eleanor.

In the fall of 1904, Franklin enrolled at Columbia Law School to be near Eleanor. They formally announced their engagement in late November 1904.

Their wedding took place on St. Patrick's Day, March 17, 1905, at the home of one of Eleanor's cousins in New York City. Reverend Endicott Peabody, Franklin's headmaster from Groton, performed the service. After appearing in the St. Patrick's Day parade, President

Roosevelt with Eleanor Roosevelt at Campobello in August 1904, shortly before they announced their engagement.

Theodore Roosevelt came to give away the bride. He told Franklin, "There's nothing like keeping the name in the family."[4] The president wound up stealing attention away from the bride and groom because of his lively presence and fame.

The couple delayed their honeymoon so that Franklin could finish his first year at Columbia Law School. Then in June 1905, they toured Europe for nearly four months. When Eleanor and Franklin returned to New York from their honeymoon, they moved into a small house on East Thirty-sixth Street. Sara had rented and furnished it in their absence and hired a full staff of servants.

This was only the first of many times that Sara Roosevelt exerted her influence on Eleanor and Franklin's marriage.[5] She also manipulated the couple's finances. Franklin and Eleanor both had trust funds inherited from their deceased parents, but these funds were too meager to support their lifestyle. Sara Roosevelt covered the expenses their trust funds did not. She could have given her son some of the money and property he would inherit when she died. But Sara preferred to retain control and give out financial gifts when she felt they were needed.[6]

On May 3, 1906, Franklin and Eleanor's first child, a daughter named Anna, was born. That summer, the family vacationed on Campobello Island. They lived with Sara, who maintained firm control over running the household.

Franklin passed the New York State Bar exam in the spring of 1907 without finishing his courses at Columbia. This practice was common among attorneys at the time. He went to work for the respected Wall Street law firm of Carter, Ledyard, and Milburn.

The Roosevelts soon had a second child, a son, James, who was born on December 23, 1907. James nearly died of pneumonia in the spring of 1908, but gradually his health improved.

In the autumn of 1908, the family moved to a larger townhouse on East Sixty-fifth Street. Sara had it built for them, right next to her own townhouse. One day soon after they had moved in, Franklin came home to find Eleanor crying. Between sobs, she explained it was not truly her house, since she had not helped to plan it.[7] Franklin could not understand why Eleanor had not voiced her opinions sooner. He quickly left the room, leaving his wife to her misery. To make matters worse, Sara Roosevelt had built the townhouses with connecting doors. Eleanor later wrote that she was "never quite sure when she [Sara] would appear, day or night."[8]

On March 18, 1909, a second son, Franklin D. Roosevelt, Jr., was born. But he had breathing and heart problems and died seven months later. Both parents grieved deeply. Although she knew the feeling had no basis in fact, Eleanor felt the baby's death was her fault. She said she had not cared enough for him. That winter she made the entire family miserable with her unhappiness.[9]

SOURCE DOCUMENT

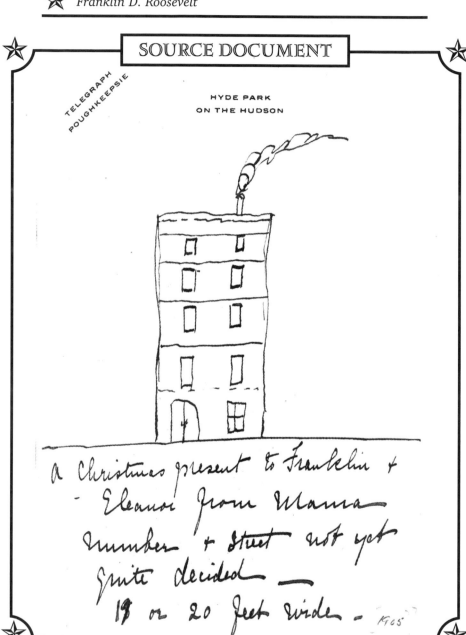

TELEGRAPH
POUGHKEEPSIE

HYDE PARK
ON THE HUDSON

*a Christmas present to Franklin +
- Eleanor from Mama
number + street not yet
quite decided —
19 or 20 feet wide —* 1905

For Christmas in 1905, Roosevelt's mother gave him and Eleanor the plans for a townhouse to be built next door to hers. It included connecting doors so that Roosevelt's mother could come and go as she pleased.

A family portrait of Eleanor, baby James, Roosevelt, and Anna taken in 1908.

Sixteen months later, on September 23, 1910, another son, Elliott, was born. He was small and sickly and temperamental as a child.[10]

By this time, Franklin Roosevelt had a plan for his political career. One day, he and five fellow law clerks discussed their goals in life. Franklin hoped to follow a similar pattern to that of Theodore Roosevelt, whom he now called Uncle Ted. Like Uncle Ted, he planned to serve in the state legislature, then become assistant secretary of the Navy, then governor of New York. He told his fellow law clerks at Carter, Ledyard, and Milburn that with "any luck," he would someday become president.[11] These were big plans for a young man not yet thirty years of age.

4

A MESSY BUSINESS

F ranklin Roosevelt got his start in politics in 1910. His mother was upset because she considered politics a "messy business."[1] Eleanor, however, supported him. Like his father, Roosevelt joined the Democratic party, even though most wealthy Americans were Republicans. Perhaps Roosevelt's choice indicated sharp political planning. He would have a better opportunity for a leadership role with the Democrats.

Party leaders considered Roosevelt a man of great promise. He had a famous name, an attractive personality, and money to finance his campaign. Party officials asked him to run for New York state senator from the 26th Senatorial District. It included Dutchess County where Springwood was located. Roosevelt was not expected to win, because no Democrat had been elected from the district since 1856. Most voters in the district were farmers, who might not trust such a well-to-do candidate. But Democratic party officials felt that the campaign would give Roosevelt excellent training for the future.

From the start, Roosevelt showed his enthusiasm and originality. He rented a bright red Maxwell touring car and covered two thousand miles campaigning. Whenever he saw a farmer, he stopped the car and visited with him. At that time, campaigning by car was unusual. He traveled at what was considered a dangerous speed—twenty-two miles per hour. The car hit a dog and scared several horses.

Each day, Roosevelt gave as many as ten speeches. Long pauses made his speaking style sound somewhat nervous. Nevertheless, he established a bond with audiences by addressing them as "my friends."[2] He supported conservation and the needs of the farmers in northern, or upstate, New York. In opposing corruption, he emphasized his relationship with Theodore Roosevelt. However, he showed little interest in the sort of social change that later made him famous as president. On election night, Franklin Roosevelt came away the surprise winner.

Eleanor and Franklin Roosevelt moved to Albany, New York, the state capital. At the time, most legislators stayed in hotels or boardinghouses. But the Roosevelts rented a three-story house well-suited to entertaining. They soon became a popular couple in Albany. Visitors were always welcomed into their home, frequently the site of stimulating dinner discussions.

Twenty-eight-year-old Franklin Roosevelt immediately showed a keen awareness of political processes. He led a group of Democrats rebelling against the powerful New York party bosses, known as Tammany Hall. Party bosses were strong and sometimes corrupt politicians who controlled votes and legislation in their party. At that time, United States senators were still chosen by the state legislature, not by the general voting public. Roosevelt's name became nationally known for supporting the direct election of senators and for working against party bosses.[3] However, Roosevelt's group eventually had to accept a candidate who was agreeable both to them and to Tammany Hall. Thus, Roosevelt learned a political lesson for the future about the need for compromise with those in power. The public remembered him as someone who worked for clean government and against party bosses.

In 1912, Roosevelt won reelection to the state legislature without making a single campaign appearance. He was ill with typhoid fever, which he caught from brushing his teeth in impure water. Roosevelt hired former newspaper reporter Louis Howe to run his campaign. Howe was a small, untidy man, but he was a tireless worker, skilled in public relations. He sent thousands of letters on Roosevelt's behalf to the farmers in the 26th District.

After their first meeting, Howe was convinced

Roosevelt might one day be president of the United States.[4] Howe respected Roosevelt's independence and courage. He saw how his boss appealed both to his campaign workers and to the voters. Howe wanted to be connected to someone with a chance to win in politics. After the 1912 campaign, he remained Roosevelt's top advisor and close friend.

In 1912, Roosevelt made another key political decision. He supported New Jersey governor Woodrow Wilson's campaign for the Democratic presidential nomination. After Wilson was elected, Roosevelt was named assistant secretary of the Navy. His idol, Theodore Roosevelt, had also once held this position. Franklin Roosevelt was only thirty-one years old, but already he had met his first two political goals on the road to becoming president.

Serving as assistant secretary of the Navy fulfilled Roosevelt's long-held dream to be a part of the United States Navy. He loved the seventeen-gun salute he received whenever he stepped onto the deck of a Navy vessel. He even designed his own assistant secretary flag to be flown when he was on board. Navy officers were impressed with his knowledge of sailing and naval history.

Roosevelt's duties included supervising the civilian employees and the operation of the Navy Department. He negotiated contracts for the purchase of coal, steel, and oil. Once, when a new submarine sank, Roosevelt went out in another submarine to show the nation that

Roosevelt successfully followed the same political path as his cousin Theodore Roosevelt, whom he idolized. Here Franklin wears gold pince-nez glasses just like those worn by his cousin.

he still supported submarine warfare. The books he read as a boy had instilled in him a love of the sea. He believed in Admiral Alfred T. Mahan's theories of sea power, which advocated the use of a large navy to gain territory and power. However, Secretary of the Navy Josephus Daniels and President Wilson were both more cautious, so Roosevelt clashed with them on this issue.

The family now lived in a Washington, D.C., home, which they rented from Roosevelt's aunt. Roosevelt liked the fact that Teddy Roosevelt had lived there just before his inauguration as president in 1901. Each morning, Roosevelt greeted his children, "Hello, chicks."[5] After a hearty breakfast, he walked to work.

In the summer of 1914, Roosevelt temporarily left his assistant secretary position to campaign as the anti-Tammany Hall candidate for the United States Senate. However, the party bosses were too powerful, and Roosevelt was soundly defeated. He returned to his position of assistant secretary of the Navy just as World War I broke out. Germany and Austria-Hungary (the Central Powers) fought against Great Britain, France, and Russia (the Allies).

Amid these tense times, the Roosevelts welcomed another member into their family. On August 17, 1914, the second Franklin Delano Roosevelt, Jr., was born.

President Wilson hoped to keep the United States out of war. But on May 7, 1915, a German submarine, or U-boat, torpedoed and sank the *Lusitania*, a British cruise ship sailing off the Irish coast. President Wilson protested strongly, because nearly twelve hundred civilians, including 128 Americans, died. Not a single soldier was on board. President Wilson decided to support an American military buildup, in preparation for possible war. Roosevelt, who had long supported preparedness, was delighted.

The Roosevelts' last child, John, was born on March 13, 1916. The Roosevelt family now included five children, four boys and one girl.

That same year, Woodrow Wilson was reelected on the campaign slogan "He kept us out of war."[6] But by

1917, relations with Germany had deteriorated further. German submarines began attacking American ships. On April 6, 1917, President Wilson went to Congress to ask for a declaration of war. He felt it was crucial that "the world be made safe for democracy."[7]

With America's entrance into World War I, Roosevelt was busier than ever. He said, "I get my fingers into everything and there's no law against it."[8] He handled recruiting and training of Navy personnel. When Roosevelt discovered that not all seamen could swim, he ordered new recruits to pass a swimming test before they could be promoted to ensign rank. Roosevelt also increased shipyard efficiency and lowered the costs of shipbuilding. He was not afraid to try out new ideas, such as a two hundred forty-mile barrier of mines laid across the North Sea.

Despite his active administrative role, Roosevelt yearned to serve in uniform in the Navy. President Wilson and Secretary of the Navy Daniels refused his request. They felt he was of more use to his country as assistant secretary. However, they sent Roosevelt on an official European inspection tour in the summer of 1918. He was close enough to the line of battle to be under fire several times. The horror of the battlefields, with thousands of graves marked with rough wooden crosses, made an impression on him. What he saw caused him to declare later that he hated war.[9]

After the Armistice, or peace agreement, was reached, Roosevelt went to Europe to supervise the disposal of naval property. On the return voyage, President Wilson shared his plans for the League of Nations, an international organization to help prevent future wars. Roosevelt became a firm supporter of the organization. However, Wilson's hope for United States membership in the League was not to be. Americans were tired of war. On September 25, 1919, Wilson collapsed while giving a speech in support of the League. Without the president's leadership, the United States Senate eventually voted against joining the League of Nations.

Assistant Secretary of the Navy Roosevelt inspected naval operations during World War I. Here, on August 14, 1918, he visited the United States Naval Air Station at Pauillac, France.

In the fall of 1918 a crisis in Roosevelt's marriage could have destroyed his chances in politics. When he returned from his first European trip, he had influenza and pneumonia. His wife, who was helping him with his correspondence, came across a group of love letters from Lucy Mercer, a young woman who had served as Eleanor Roosevelt's social secretary. With the discovery of these letters, Eleanor wrote, "The bottom dropped out of my own particular world. . . ."[10] She had based her developing self-confidence on what seemed to be her solid relationship with her husband. Now she was devastated and offered Roosevelt a divorce. If he did not break off with Lucy, Eleanor said she would insist on divorce.[11] Some historians also believe that Sara Roosevelt threatened to discontinue any financial help to her son if he did not give up Lucy Mercer.[12] Roosevelt and Mercer promised never to see each other again.

Eleanor and Franklin Roosevelt agreed to stay together, but their relationship changed. No longer were they romantically close, although they showed affection toward their children. Their partnership became a more businesslike one. In fact, they developed into one of the most effective married political teams in history.

Roosevelt entered the world of national politics in 1920. The Democrats selected Governor James M. Cox of Ohio as their presidential candidate and thirty-eight-year-old Franklin Roosevelt as his running mate. Although he was young, Roosevelt had already achieved national notice. Since he was from New York, Roosevelt brought geographical balance to the ticket. The Republican nominee for president, Warren G. Harding, promised a return to "normalcy."[13]

Traditionally, the vice-presidential candidate did not actively campaign. However, Roosevelt was determined to be involved. He traveled hundreds of miles by train, giving as many as one thousand speeches. He and Cox based their campaign on America's possible entrance into the League of Nations. However, most Americans were not interested in this issue.

In 1920, women were given the right to vote, so a candidate's wife would now play an important campaign role. She would exert a huge influence on new, female voters. Eleanor agreed to join Franklin, even though she disliked campaigning. Louis Howe soon recognized her intelligence, organization, and energy. He began to compliment Eleanor on these qualities, which helped build the foundation for the Roosevelts' strong political partnership.

Despite Roosevelt's enthusiastic campaigning, Harding won the presidency. Roosevelt was disappointed, but realistic. He knew he had gained valuable campaign experience as well as tremendous national exposure. He never lost interest in developing an international peacekeeping organization and followed up on this idea when he became president.

After the election, Roosevelt worked as a vice-president of the Fidelity and Deposit Company of Maryland in their New York office. Fidelity and Deposit insured companies against risks of loss from theft or bankruptcy. They paid him twenty-five thousand dollars a year, five times his salary as assistant secretary of the Navy. This welcome increase in salary helped pay the high fees charged by the private schools his children attended. Roosevelt also formed a law partnership. Mornings, he worked at Fidelity and Deposit. Afternoons, he crossed the street and worked in his law office.

He also explored a variety of private business ventures. They included placing advertisements in taxicabs and setting up vending machines to sell products. Both of these were considered novel ideas at the time. In his spare time, he also headed the Navy Club and the Greater New York Boy Scout Council. In all his ventures, he showed the enthusiasm and willingness to experiment that became characteristic of his political career.

In the meantime, Roosevelt kept up his correspondence with political supporters. Several news reporters observed that during the 1920 election, he had acted more like the presidential candidate than had Governor Cox.[14] He was one of the leading Democrats in the nation. It was assumed that he just had to maintain his position, and he was sure to be elected president in the next election. But something unforeseen occurred. It was an attack of polio.

5

A CHALLENGING TIME

After losing the election of 1920, Roosevelt told a friend that the moment of defeat was the best time to make plans for future Democratic victories.[1] But in 1921, his polio attack forced him to adapt his plans. The experience could have crushed a person with less determination. In the case of Franklin Roosevelt, he refused to let his disability stand in the way of his plans.

From the beginning of Roosevelt's illness, his campaign manager, Louis Howe, had concealed the seriousness of his condition from newspaper reporters. Howe first described it as a "bad cold" and later reported that Roosevelt's health had improved.[2] In the 1920s, society in general shunned the handicapped. Because of people's ignorance, the disabled were often blamed for their own poor condition.[3] It was assumed Roosevelt's political career would be jeopardized if the public found out about his paralysis.

Four weeks after his polio attack, Roosevelt felt strong enough to be transferred from Campobello Island to New York's Presbyterian Hospital. After Roosevelt arrived at the hospital, reporters learned that he had polio. But Howe led the reporters to believe that Roosevelt would not be permanently crippled.[4]

When Roosevelt was discharged from the hospital in October, he still could not sit up without help. His hospital record noted that he was "not improving."[5] At his New York townhouse, he started exercises that he hoped would restore his ability to walk. He pulled himself along the floor, using his arms. Sitting up, he crept backward, dragging his limp, frail legs behind him. Roosevelt said heavyweight boxing champion Jack Dempsey would envy the strong shoulder and chest muscles he had developed.[6]

Roosevelt's mother began to pressure her son to stop his involvement in politics. She believed that polio would now force him to retire to the estate in Hyde Park. Sara had control of the estate and the money she had inherited from her husband. Having her son at Springwood would allow her to maintain control over his life again.

Eleanor Roosevelt and Louis Howe took the opposite position. They felt Roosevelt's morale depended on his return to politics.[7] Howe encouraged Eleanor Roosevelt to become active in the Democratic party. As a result, she brought key officials and interesting people to visit her husband. In so doing, she kept the Roosevelt name in the forefront of the party. Eleanor refused to treat her husband as helpless and forbade others from doing so.

However, Roosevelt's relationship with his children did change. Previously, he had been strong and active. After the polio attack, the children watched him struggle to regain his health and his career. Now, suddenly, he needed them. He had to be lifted in and out of automobiles. He needed a strong arm to lean on when he learned to walk with braces and a cane. His reliance on the help of his two oldest sons, James and Elliott, increased their self-esteem. (However, none of the children ever duplicated their father's success. As adults, the five Roosevelt children experienced numerous job failures and twenty divorces among them.)

Despite the support of Roosevelt's family, the atmosphere in their home became increasingly stressful. Sara Roosevelt, who lived in the adjoining townhouse, was a constant visitor. She often complained about the presence of Louis Howe, who had moved in to help care for his boss. Four of the five Roosevelt children were living at home. They also disliked having Howe there. Fifteen-year-old Anna resented his presence, because he occupied the bedroom that had been hers. Sara encouraged the children to express their frustration. Eleanor and Sara Roosevelt continued to argue over Roosevelt's rehabilitation.

Many family members and friends have insisted that Roosevelt never felt depressed about his condition.[8] In public situations and with his family, especially his children, he consistently showed a strong sense of optimism. Dr. Ross McIntire, who was his physician when Roosevelt was president, wrote that "no one ever saw him indulge in so much as a moment of self-pity."[9] Roosevelt's secretary, Marguerite "Missy" LeHand, held a different view. She maintained that some days it was noon before Roosevelt could pull himself out of his depression.[10] Years later, Roosevelt told Frances Perkins, who served on his presidential Cabinet, that he had often felt depressed. He said that during the first days of his illness, his despair was so deep that he thought God had deserted him.[11]

As Christmas 1921 approached, Roosevelt became stronger. However, when James came home from Groton for the holiday, he broke into tears at the sight of his previously active father lying in bed. Roosevelt reassured him with a huge smile—and defeated James in every one of their arm-wrestling contests.

Unfortunately, in January 1922, Roosevelt's weakened leg muscles contracted, so that his legs bent nearly backward. Both legs were put into plaster casts. Wedges were painfully driven deeper and deeper into the casts to stretch the muscles.

In February 1922, Roosevelt's doctors fitted him with leather and steel leg braces. They weighed seven pounds each and locked at his knees. By balancing himself on crutches and swinging his hips, Roosevelt was able to perform a crude sort of walk.

In the summer of 1922, Roosevelt moved to Springwood. Each day, he worked out on parallel bars. He pulled his paralyzed body along by leaning on his arms and alternately shifting forward on them. He also walked down the estate's quarter-mile-long driveway with his crutches and leg braces. When he fell, he had to wait for someone to come help him up. He also spent hours swimming in the indoor heated pool of his neighbor, Vincent Astor. Roosevelt said, "Water got me into this fix! Water will get me out again!"[12]

That winter, he chartered a houseboat and cruised the warm Florida seas for several weeks. Swimming in the balmy saltwater made Roosevelt's legs feel better. His sons James and Elliott joined him for part of their school vacations. Roosevelt spent the next three winters cruising on a houseboat. These restful periods gave him confidence that his health would continue to improve. Then he could return to politics.

But political leaders sought him out sooner than he had planned. In 1924, Roosevelt's friend, Al Smith, decided to run for president of the United States. He asked Roosevelt to give his nomination speech at the Democratic National Convention.

Roosevelt's sixteen-year-old son, James, served as his assistant. They had practiced a way of walking that would make Roosevelt look as strong as possible. He used James's arm for support on one side and a crutch on the other. He gripped his son's arm so tightly at times that James struggled to keep from crying out.[13] When Roosevelt reached the end of the aisle, his son handed him his other crutch. By slowly swinging his legs back and forth while shifting his crutches, Roosevelt inched his way to the podium.

Finally, Roosevelt reached the podium and began speaking in a clear, confident voice. His famous smile blazed out at the delegates. Roosevelt praised Smith as a sincere leader, the "happy warrior of the political battlefield."[14] Columnist Walter Lippmann termed the speech "moving and distinguished."[15]

Smith, however, did not earn the presidential nomination. The defeat actually worked in Roosevelt's favor. With the Republicans in power, Democrats like Roosevelt had little chance for election. Roosevelt returned to his program of exercises and tried a new therapy. On October 24, 1924, he visited Warm Springs, a run-down health spa in Georgia. Roosevelt loved the warmth of the mineral waters, which flowed from a natural pool under nearby Pine Mountain. He could even stand and walk unassisted in the pool.

He was so enthused about the resort that he purchased it in 1926. Roosevelt's influence drew many patients. Calling himself "Dr. Roosevelt," he loved to encourage them in their exercises. He also enjoyed driving through the surrounding countryside in his car. It had a special set of hand controls to operate the brakes and gas pedal. He often stopped to visit with his neighbors.

The Roosevelt children were getting older. James entered Harvard in 1926, but Elliott flunked his Harvard entrance exams on purpose and refused to go to college. Anna married stockbroker Curtis Dall. In 1927, she presented Franklin and Eleanor with their first grandchild, Curtis.

That same year, Roosevelt formed the Georgia Warm Springs Foundation, a nonprofit organization. It could receive grants and tax-free gifts for the resort's redevelopment. Eventually, Roosevelt used two thirds of his own fortune to renovate Warm Springs. He built himself a small cottage on the grounds. Later, when he became president, it was known as the Little White House. An unusual feature for that time was its seven telephone jacks.

The following year, Al Smith again decided to run for president. Again, he asked Roosevelt to give the nomination speech. This time, Roosevelt's eighteen-year-old son, Elliott, helped him walk to the speakers' platform. Elliott, with his history of behavior problems, was pleased to receive this attention from his father. For the first time, the nomination speech would also be heard on the radio. Roosevelt seemed to sense the importance of radio for future campaigns.[16] He spoke smoothly and confidently.

In order to win, Smith had to carry the large states, such as his home state of New York. It would help if one

Roosevelt relaxes at his cottage in Warm Springs, Georgia, which later became known as the Little White House. He bought the health-spa resort in 1926.

of his supporters ran for governor there. He asked Roosevelt to run. But Roosevelt did not want to stop his therapy. Louis Howe opposed Roosevelt's candidacy, because he felt Smith and most Democrats would lose in 1928. Therefore, Howe reasoned a loss could hurt Roosevelt's future political chances. However, Smith finally convinced Roosevelt to run.

His health was a campaign issue from the start. Smith retorted, "We don't elect a Governor for his ability to do a double back flip or a handspring. The work of the Governorship is brain work."[17] Roosevelt set out to prove his stamina. He gave more speeches in more locations than had any prior candidate for New York governor. At the start of a speech, he listed the places at which he had spoken recently. Then he replied with sarcasm, "Too bad about this unfortunate sick man, isn't it?"[18]

He traveled over thirteen hundred miles in a month of campaigning. He often spoke from the backseat of an open automobile. It had a steel bar mounted over the seat. Roosevelt would pull himself up using the bar and lock his leg braces in place. After speaking, he would unlock the braces and sit down.

Despite Roosevelt's assurances, the demands of campaigning were difficult. He did not want to be viewed in a wheelchair or with crutches. Transporting him from one campaign location to the next without being seen was difficult. Once he was carried up a fire escape to reach a stage.[19] On another night, a fire escape also appeared to be the only way to reach the auditorium unseen. But this fire escape was too narrow to allow Roosevelt to be carried. He finally had to drag himself up the stairs, using only his arms.

Despite Roosevelt's supportive campaign, Smith lost to Herbert Hoover in 1928. But Roosevelt was a surprise victor. He won the governorship by twenty-five thousand votes out of 4.25 million cast. He was sworn in on January 1, 1929, in the same room as Theodore Roosevelt had been thirty years before. Franklin Roosevelt had taken another step in his goal to reach the presidency.

The governor's mansion was quickly modified for Roosevelt's use. Ramps were placed over the steps. A pool was installed in the backyard for his exercises. The mansion immediately became a scene of bustling activity. The four Roosevelt sons were constantly in and out. The Roosevelts' daughter, Anna, now had two children and visited often. Louis Howe also had a bedroom in the mansion. In addition, the nine guest rooms were usually full.

Eleanor Roosevelt spent part of the week in Albany and the remainder in New York City. She taught three days a week at Todhunter School, which she had purchased with a friend. Her influence on her husband increased. She wrote him letters of advice on issues and political appointees. When she learned of a book she thought her husband should read, she left it on his bedside table. Eleanor also served as his eyes and ears on inspection tours of state facilities. He would be carried to a car and driven to the hospital or another state institution. Then Eleanor would closely examine conditions inside and describe them to her husband.

Roosevelt went right to work on issues facing New York state. He was the first governor to back unemployment insurance and tax relief to farmers. His support of cheap electrical power appealed to consumers. He improved the judicial system and the prisons. Serving as governor provided Roosevelt with excellent administrative experience.

A key element of his success was the use of radio. At

the time, most newspapers supported the Republicans. Roosevelt used the radio to address the voters directly, speaking like one friend to another. Later, as president, he successfully used this same approach with his Fireside Chats.

Events of October 1929 changed the nation's view of President Hoover and the Republican party. Throughout the 1920s, the United States economy thrived. Wages were high. For the first time, people bought household goods, such as refrigerators, on credit. The stock market seemed like an ideal opportunity to get rich quick. Between 1923 and 1929, stock prices rose nearly 200 percent. Many people borrowed money to buy stocks.

On October 29, 1929, now commonly known as Black Tuesday, the stock market crashed. Millions of investors tried to sell their stocks, but no one wanted to buy. Prices dropped until many stocks were worthless. Those who had borrowed money to buy stocks could not pay their debts. The crash triggered a panic. People rushed to their banks to withdraw their funds. Banks lost huge amounts in the crash and could not pay their depositors. These banks closed, and many depositors lost their life savings.

The stock market crash marked the beginning of the Great Depression, the worst economic period in United States history. Between 1929 and 1933, approximately ten thousand banks closed. Factories cut back on production, which put people out of work. By 1933, 13 million people were jobless. Those without jobs had no money to spend, so the economy could not improve. At this time, most European countries had unemployment insurance to help workers who lost their jobs. But no such system existed in the United States. Workers lost confidence in the economic system and in their government's ability to help.

President Hoover believed the economy would correct itself. He felt individual Americans should rely on themselves and their families, not on the government, for help. Hoover did ask Congress for limited funds for federal public works programs. But he was unwilling to spend enough of the government's funds to cure the severe economic woes.

At first, Governor Roosevelt agreed with Herbert Hoover that the economy would heal itself. From 1929 to 1930, he proposed only limited public assistance in New York. But information from staff members changed Roosevelt's outlook. He became convinced that the economy was getting worse. In August 1931, he created the Temporary Emergency Relief Administration (TERA), the first unemployment relief agency created by a state.

The Republicans had claimed credit for the good times of the 1920s. Now they carried the blame for the Great Depression. People waited in long breadlines. "Hoovervilles"—settlements of people living in shacks, old cars, and packing boxes—sprang up near dumps and in vacant lots. As the economy collapsed, Roosevelt's political fortunes grew. He was reelected governor in 1930. Will Rogers, the cowboy humorist, said, "The Democrats nominated their President yesterday, Franklin D. Roosevelt."[20] Many newspapers were now predicting that Roosevelt would be elected president in 1932.[21]

Roosevelt continued his work as governor, but also formed a presidential campaign organization under the direction of Louis Howe and James Farley. Farley headed the Democratic party in New York. He was known for his charming manner. His ability to remember names and faces was extremely useful in politics. Roosevelt also gathered a group of college professors who came to be known as his "brain trust." He questioned and debated issues with this group.

In June 1932, the Democratic National Convention nominated Roosevelt on the fourth ballot. He immediately flew to the convention in Chicago to accept the nomination. Although he disliked flying, he wanted to show voters that he was ready for vigorous action. The ride on the cold, tiny, trimotor plane was bumpy. Roosevelt's son John was sick to his stomach in the back of the plane. But Roosevelt seemed calm. He revised his acceptance speech and then was relaxed enough to nap.

Cheering crowds welcomed him to the convention. His speech outlined the action he intended to take. He said, "I pledge you, I pledge myself, to a new deal for the American people. . . ."[22] The words *new deal* became forever tied to Franklin D. Roosevelt.

6

THE NEW DEAL

T he main campaign issue in 1932 was the depression. In a radio talk in April, Roosevelt called for an economy built on the foundation of "the forgotten man at the bottom of the economic pyramid."[1] The "forgotten man" became one of his most famous phrases. Roosevelt criticized Hoover for being too conservative in his use of government power to stop the economic decline. Throughout the campaign, Hoover seemed stern and uncomfortable. Roosevelt campaigned with his typical enthusiasm. He loved giving speeches and going out to meet voters. Roosevelt won the election by 7 million votes and carried forty-two of the forty-eight states. His new vice-president was John Garner, a congressman from Texas and Speaker of the House of Representatives.

At that time, the presidential election took place in November, but the inauguration did not occur until the following March.[2] Between the election and the inauguration, the economy declined drastically. Americans felt an increasing sense of panic. Herbert Hoover offered no hope. He said, "We are at the end of our string. There is nothing more we can do."[3]

The nation's confidence suffered another jolt on February 15, 1933. Roosevelt had just finished giving a speech in Miami, Florida, when Joseph Zangara, an unemployed plumber, tried to assassinate him. The plumber's shots missed the newly elected president, but killed Chicago mayor Anton Cernak. Roosevelt remained calm throughout the incident. Such behavior was typical of how calmly he faced crises after his attack of polio.

On the morning of the inauguration, March 4, all banks and the New York Stock Exchange were closed. Franklin Roosevelt took the oath of office with his right hand placed on his Dutch family Bible. Then he spoke out in a strong, clear voice. Roosevelt believed that fear gripped the nation. Recovery was impossible until that fear was removed. He projected optimism when he said, "the only thing we have to fear is fear itself."[4] Citizens needed jobs so that they could regain their self-respect, as well as earn a living wage. He pledged, "This nation asks for action, and action now. Our primary task is to put people to work."[5] He gave the American public great hope with this promise. Roosevelt also pledged strict supervision of all banking and investments.

Eleanor Roosevelt showed a sense of optimism and enthusiasm equal to her husband's. Some people criticized Eleanor, because a first lady had never before worked or been so active.[6] She was a highly paid lecturer and wrote articles on education and family concerns, donating the money to causes she supported. Eleanor also owned a furniture-making business. She served as her husband's "listening post" so that he could receive a balanced picture of the country's opinions.[7] Eleanor also held press conferences, another first for first ladies. Political questions were not allowed, because she did not want to interfere with the president's business.[8]

Cozy furniture, some of it from Hyde Park, filled the living quarters on the second floor of the White House. Fala, Roosevelt's black Scottish terrier, slept on a chair in his master's bedroom. Teen-aged Franklin, Jr., and John kept late hours. Eleanor told the White House guards to let them in no matter how late they returned. Anna and her two children often stayed at the White House. (Anna was now separated from her husband.)

Roosevelt, now commonly known as FDR, woke each morning between eight and nine. He had breakfast in bed and read several newspapers. He was a fast reader with a tremendous memory for detail. The president met with staff members and then got dressed. He took the elevator to his downstairs office, arriving about 10:30 A.M. His desk was decorated with collections of miniature donkeys, elephants, and Scottie dogs.

To get about, Roosevelt used a special wheelchair. It

was cut down from an ordinary, straight-backed wooden kitchen chair. There were no arms on the chair, so he could slide easily from the wheelchair to a couch, desk chair, or the seat of his car.

Roosevelt's secretary, Missy LeHand, managed his busy schedule and correspondence. Once a week, he held Cabinet meetings and met with John Garner, his vice-president. His press conferences usually occurred two times a week. Each day, his appointments were scheduled about fifteen minutes apart. But FDR often strayed from his schedule. He kept some visitors longer. He used conversation to manipulate his interviews. Sometimes he did not want to hear what the visitor had to say. Other times he had not made up his mind about whatever the speaker had come to ask about. Then FDR would keep telling stories and anecdotes until the appointment time was up. Some visitors felt cheated, because they thought he had not paid attention to their concerns.[9]

FDR used his conversational style to avoid arguments or confrontation. He nodded his head while listening. His visitor assumed FDR agreed, but this was not necessarily so. FDR's nod just meant that he was paying attention.[10]

Depending on his workload, FDR sometimes went for a drive around 4:00 P.M. Or he went to the family quarters for tea. Even when he had more work to do, he usually left his office by 5:30. Most days, he swam in the White House pool. Children across the nation had

> SOURCE DOCUMENT

This cartoon shows FDR's famous pose, with his chin up and clenching a cigarette holder in his teeth.

contributed dimes and nickels to build the pool. FDR relaxed with cocktails before dinner.

After dinner, FDR took time off if he had no more work to do. Two or three times a week, he watched a movie in the White House movie theater. In his second-floor study, he enjoyed poring over his stamp collection or playing poker. Before going to sleep, he often read several pages of a mystery book or a thriller.

When FDR went anywhere, he was never photographed getting in or out of a wheelchair. He was so highly regarded by the press that they honored this unwritten agreement. Most Americans remained unaware that he even needed a wheelchair.

Before a presidential visit, the Secret Service would prepare the location ahead of time by building ramps. On occasion, they raised the entire level of a street to match the level of a building. A wooden framework supported ramps and platforms strong enough to hold the president's car. The car was driven up the ramps to the building. The president could then "walk" more directly into the building from his car.

The first weeks of Roosevelt's administration are often called the "Hundred Days."[11] During this time, a record amount of legislation was passed. Every few days, FDR sent a proposal to Congress aimed at stopping the Great Depression and providing work. If an idea did not work, he tried something new. He admitted that he expected to make mistakes.[12] The agencies and policies he developed during his first term came to be known collectively as the "New Deal."

FDR began by attacking the banking crisis. He declared a bank holiday and closed all banks. Some never reopened. FDR called a special session of Congress to approve his proposal, the Emergency Banking Act. The bill called for the Treasury Department to investigate each bank. Those with enough funds would be allowed to reopen right away.

On March 12, 1933, during his first week in office, FDR gave his first radio address to reassure the nation. These national broadcasts were called Fireside Chats because he pretended he was talking to a few people sitting around his fireplace.[13] In this first "chat," he described his plan to restore health to the ailing banking system. He used simple terms and spoke in a calm, reassuring voice. The talk was a huge success. His mother, who now supported his political career, listened to every one of these Fireside Chats. "Good!" or "How true that is!" she would comment, as if he were speaking just to her.[14]

FDR also held his first press conference that week. He started a new procedure. Reporters did not have to

Roosevelt delivered his first Fireside Chat over the radio at the end of the bank holiday on March 12, 1933. The "chat" was broadcast directly from the White House.

turn in their questions beforehand. FDR appeared comfortable as the reporters peppered him with their questions. He also asked the public to share their ideas with him. Thousands of letters flooded the White House. They went into his "bedtime folder," and he read them at night or early in the morning.[15] Both the first Fireside Chat and press conference immediately calmed Americans.

Next, FDR tackled the problems facing the economy. The Federal Emergency Relief Act (FERA) passed in 1933 and set aside $500 million of relief money for unemployed workers. Created under FERA, the Civil Works Administration (CWA) provided jobs for more than 4 million people. It hired the unemployed to build parks, roads, post offices, schools, and libraries.

The Civilian Conservation Corps (CCC) was FDR's favorite relief program. Young men were recruited from the cities, where unemployment was high. They lived in camps built by the War Department. Roosevelt called the CCC his civilian "tree army."[16] "He loved trees," said Secretary of Labor Frances Perkins, "and he hated to see them cut and not replaced."[17] The CCC also restocked lakes and streams with fish and improved national parks, beaches, and campgrounds.

Farmers also needed help. Their income had dropped severely in the 1920s compared with the wages of factory workers. By the mid-1930s, drought blew away much of the rich topsoil in the Midwest. Thick dust clouds called black blizzards turned the whole area

Roosevelt (middle of bottom row) with his first Cabinet. Frances Perkins, on the right in the back row, served as secretary of labor. She was the first woman to serve on any Cabinet.

into what was called the Dust Bowl.[18] Many farmers could not make their mortgage payments and lost their farms. Those who were able to continue farming grew too many crops. The surplus then caused prices to drop. Farmers began to leave their crops in the field to rot or burned them as fuel, since the price of coal was so high. Starving city dwellers could not understand why the farmers were disposing of food.

In May 1933, FDR addressed these problems with the Agricultural Adjustment Act (AAA). The AAA limited farm production by paying farmers to grow certain crops. It also paid them if they did not plant part of their fields. The purpose of this action was to keep a portion of the soil fertile for the following season's planting. As a result, certain crops would be scarcer. If a crop was scarce, its price went up. This helped farmers make more money. By earning more, farmers were able to make their farm mortgage payments. Unfortunately, since many Americans were unemployed, they could

SOURCE DOCUMENT

In this political cartoon, Dr. New Deal (Roosevelt) proposes a variety of remedies to the nurse (Congress) to help heal Uncle Sam (the United States).

not afford to buy food. It also seemed wrong to have farmers cut production when many Americans did not have enough to eat.

One of the poorest farm regions in the nation was the Tennessee Valley, where the soil had been exhausted by overuse. The Tennessee Valley Authority (TVA) was established in May 1933. It built five dams and improved twenty others to control river flooding and generate cheap electrical power. The TVA program was criticized as "socialistic." Socialism advocates a high level of government control of industry and no private ownership of property. The people of the Tennessee Valley, however, were happy to have electrical power and a chance to prosper.

In 1933, FDR formed the Federal Deposit Insurance Corporation (FDIC), which still operates today. The FDIC insured the value of bank deposits, which renewed investors' confidence in banks.

The National Industrial Recovery Act (NIRA) established the right to collective bargaining, or having a union represent workers. The NIRA created the Public Works Administration (PWA). Between 1935 and 1941, the PWA employed about 2 million workers on construction projects such as highways, dams, and hospitals. PWA projects included New York's Lincoln Tunnel and the University of New Mexico library.

An important but unsuccessful section of the NIRA was the National Recovery Administration (NRA). It set nationwide standards for maximum working hours and minimum wages. It also established codes, or standards, for businesses. These codes were so precise that enforcing them was difficult. For example, one code forbade packaging egg noodles in yellow wrapping, since this would make them look more nutritious than they actually were.[19]

The Securities and Exchange Commission (SEC) registered all stocks traded on the stock exchange. It required corporations to supply information on their company to stock purchasers. The SEC still exists today.

The first New Deal programs created strong public support for FDR. They helped control the chaos in United States banking and finance, but they did not cure the Great Depression. By 1934, opposition to the level of government control had increased. In August, the American Liberty League formed. Its members, many of America's wealthiest citizens, refused to call Roosevelt by name. They referred to him as "that man in the White House."[20] In addition, by 1936 the Supreme Court had declared unconstitutional several New Deal measures, including the NRA and AAA. Roosevelt decided to propose new reforms, which were called the Second New Deal.

In the spring of 1935, the National Labor Relations Act, or Wagner Act, was signed. It required management to bargain fairly with unions. Passage of the Wagner Act resulted in a huge expansion of unions and many strikes, some of which were bloody.

New relief programs were created. The most famous

was the Works Progress Administration (WPA), which operated from 1935 to 1941. Writers composed guidebooks to American cities, states, and regions. Artists painted murals on post office walls. More than two thousand ex-slaves were interviewed and their experiences recorded. Some people criticized the WPA for "boondoggling," or developing made-up work projects.[21] But the WPA successfully employed over 8 million people.

Perhaps the most important achievement of the New Deal and certainly the most long-lasting was the Social Security Act of 1935. It provided old-age and unemployment insurance. In addition, the elderly, dependent children, and the handicapped became eligible for welfare benefits. Social Security was funded by contributions from both the employer and the employee, as it is today. Although we now take it for granted, at the time Social Security was considered an extreme idea. Critics maintained that the program made individuals too dependent on government assistance and less inclined to save money on their own.

As the 1936 election approached, Roosevelt's popularity remained high among the poor and middle-class voters. They credited him with saving their jobs. Wealthier citizens considered FDR a traitor to their social class and were almost obsessed with hatred.[22] When he attended Harvard's 300th anniversary celebration, he was booed. Well-to-do voters disliked that he had raised taxes and created a welfare system.

A Works Progress Administration (WPA) poster from the 1930s. The WPA supported more than 250,000 projects, which helped preserve America's cultural heritage. It also provided jobs for unemployed farmers and factory workers and built or renovated 110,000 public buildings.

Business leaders did not want government regulation or powerful unions.

Even so, Roosevelt was nominated unanimously at the Democratic National Convention in Philadelphia. In his acceptance speech, he announced, "We have conquered fear."[23] He felt America was waging a war against poverty and for the very survival of democracy. "This generation of Americans," he proclaimed, "has a rendezvous with destiny. . . . We are fighting to save a great and precious form of government for ourselves and for the world."[24] Vice-President John Garner was again Roosevelt's running mate.

The Republican opponent was Governor Alfred M. Landon of Kansas, who was supported by most of the nation's newspapers. But the voters backed Roosevelt. He was elected by a margin of almost 11 million votes. He carried every state but Maine and Vermont. By Inauguration Day 1937, the economic situation was vastly improved from four years before. Farm prices and factory wages were up. Unemployment was down. "I see a great nation . . . blessed with a great wealth of natural resources," FDR announced.[25] But he believed the country's economic situation was still not good enough. "I see one third of a nation ill-housed, ill-clad, ill-nourished," he said.[26] He proposed to continue leading the American people down their road to recovery.

However, he ran into a roadblock—the Supreme Court. By 1937, the Court had ruled against eleven of the sixteen cases involving New Deal measures. The justices of the Supreme Court were appointed for life, but FDR had not yet had a chance to appoint any. He sent a surprise proposal to Congress that the number of justices be increased from nine to fifteen. At various times in United States history, the size of the Court had changed. Roosevelt maintained that a younger judiciary would increase the Court's efficiency.[27] But his real goal was to appoint a majority who agreed with him. This effort at packing the Court with his supporters made FDR look power-hungry and devious. Congress rejected the plan. The defeat cost Roosevelt the support of older, powerful Democrats who had been uncertain about some parts of the New Deal. By this time, the justices had changed their opinions on some of the cases, anyway. They upheld Social Security and the Wagner Act. One justice retired, so FDR made an appointment that would assure him of a majority. Eventually, he was able to appoint eight justices, altogether. He also named Harlan F. Stone as Chief Justice. Stone had served as an associate justice of the Court since 1925.

In the spring of 1937, Roosevelt focused on balancing the budget. However, problems soon developed for the New Deal. By autumn, the economy had taken a downturn. The stock market declined. FDR's emphasis on balancing the national budget was the main cause. In April 1938, Congress approved his $6.5 billion package of loans and direct government spending.

The New Deal changed America's view of government. It is difficult to imagine society today without

Social Security, unemployment insurance, and banking regulation. Because of FDR's programs, many Americans came to depend on government to solve their economic woes. The New Deal increased federal government regulation in areas that were weak, such as the stock market and the banking system. But the New Deal did not solve the economic problems created by the Great Depression. It took World War II to restore the United States economy.

Critics accused Roosevelt of excessive government spending.

7

THREATS OF WAR

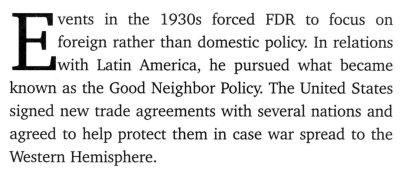

E vents in the 1930s forced FDR to focus on foreign rather than domestic policy. In relations with Latin America, he pursued what became known as the Good Neighbor Policy. The United States signed new trade agreements with several nations and agreed to help protect them in case war spread to the Western Hemisphere.

In much of the world, dictators preached imperialism, the forcible takeover of other nations. In Germany, Adolf Hitler came into power in 1932. Hitler promised to restore the German nation to its former might. The National Socialist German Workers' (Nazi) party, headed by Hitler, soon eliminated all opposition. In Italy, Benito Mussolini's Fascist party was in power and invaded Ethiopia in 1935. Germany and Italy joined together in an alliance known as the Axis.

The American people were isolationists who, after the price paid in World War I, did not want to become involved in another European war. In a public opinion poll taken in 1936, two thirds of those polled opposed any action to stop aggression.[1]

In Asia, the Japanese had conquered Manchuria in 1932 and now moved deeper into China. Roosevelt felt Japanese imperialism had to be stopped. On October 5, 1937, he gave his "Quarantine the Aggressors Speech."[2] Aggressors should be quarantined, or isolated, just as someone with a severe illness is quarantined. Such a quarantine might prevent aggression from spreading. The speech attracted so much attention that it nearly drove the World Series baseball news off the front page of national newspapers. Democratic party leaders did not support the president's position. Opinion polls taken at the time also showed that most voters were not ready for such a forceful stance.[3]

On December 12, 1937, in broad daylight, the Japanese bombed the United States gunboat *Panay* anchored in the Yangtze River in China. Two Americans died. But isolationists pressured the Roosevelt administration into accepting an apology from Japan.

In March 1938, Hitler announced union, or *Anschluss*, between Germany and Austria. This meant Austria was forced to become a province of Germany. Late that same year, the Munich Conference was held.

The leaders of Great Britain and France hoped to avoid war, so they agreed to allow Germany to occupy western Czechoslovakia. Hitler promised that he would seek to gain no additional territory.[4] In March 1939, only six months after the Munich Conference, Hitler broke the promise he made there and conquered the rest of Czechoslovakia. In an opinion poll organized by *Fortune* magazine, three fourths of Americans said they expected war to break out in Europe soon.[5]

Russian leader Joseph Stalin shocked the world in August 1939 by signing a pact with Hitler. Russia and Germany agreed not to attack each other. Stalin would have been wise to remember that Hitler had already broken the promises he made in Munich.

On September 1, 1939, a German *blitzkrieg*, or lightning war consisting of massive air power and heavy bombing, conquered Poland. Two days later, Great Britain and France, the Allies, declared war on Germany. World War II had begun.

Roosevelt immediately gave a Fireside Chat. He expected some Americans to oppose the war, some to support it. However, he stressed that the United States would not go to war.[6]

On January 4, 1940, FDR asked Congress to revise the Neutrality Acts, legislation that had been passed between 1935–1937. The acts forbade the sale of American weapons to any nation at war. They did not distinguish between the attackers, or aggressors, and their victims. FDR wanted to support the Allies by selling them arms. Congress agreed to allow the purchase of weapons by other nations on a cash-and-carry basis. The Allies had to pay cash and transport the war materiel on their own ships.

In April 1940, the Nazis conquered Denmark, Norway, the Netherlands, and Belgium. By November, they also occupied much of France. The British were now fighting the Axis powers alone. Roosevelt used an executive order to transfer fifty old but usable American destroyers to the British. In turn, the British gave the United States the right to build bases on British territory in the Western Hemisphere. By this time, United States public opinion had shifted. More than 66 percent of Americans believed that Germany now presented a direct threat to the United States.[7]

In May 1940, Congress granted FDR one billion dollars to build warplanes and increase the size of the Navy. Such military buildup concerned some Americans. In July, they formed the America First Committee. Its members protested that preparing for war would give more power to FDR and the federal government. A famous America First member, aviator Charles A. Lindbergh, felt the British were close to defeat. Thus involvement in Europe would be useless anyway.

In the meantime, the Roosevelt administration continued to prepare for possible war. In mid-September 1940, Congress approved the Selective Service Act, which established the nation's first peacetime draft. Young men ages twenty-one to thirty-six could be drafted.

That same month, Japan signed the Tripartite Pact with Germany and Italy. The three nations pledged to aid each other in case of attack. This pact was a definite threat to United States security.

FDR also faced the issue of the 1940 election. At this time, no legislation had ever been passed restricting the president to two terms. FDR was beginning to show the physical strains of holding such a stressful position. He also wanted to write his memoirs, or life story. Yet he felt a responsibility to take the nomination if the world political situation worsened. On purpose, Roosevelt never revealed his intent in public, not even to Eleanor. But he also did not withdraw his name from consideration. This made it difficult for any other Democrat to gain support. Just before the Democratic convention in July, FDR let party leaders know he was interested in running. He was immediately nominated. His vice-presidential running mate was Henry Wallace, his secretary of agriculture.

The Republicans chose Indiana businessman Wendell Willkie as their candidate. Willkie had originally been a Democrat, but after 1933, he no longer supported many New Deal policies. Willkie made the third term a campaign issue. He cautioned of the danger in having one person hold the nation's highest office for twelve years. However, FDR still won the election with 55 percent of the popular vote.

In December 1940, FDR held a White House press conference to announce a landmark policy called

Lend-Lease. He argued that the best defense for America was the ability of Great Britain to defend herself. Lend-Lease allowed the government to lend or lease ships, arms, and other war materials to any nation considered "vital to the defense of the United States."[8] Senator Burton Wheeler of Montana said that Lend-Lease stamped the president as war-minded.[9] However, Wendell Willkie, FDR's former opponent, appeared before Congress to support Lend-Lease. When asked why, he responded, "I struggled as hard as I could to beat Franklin Roosevelt. . . . He was elected President. He is my President now."[10]

At the end of December, FDR gave a Fireside Chat on national security and military aid for Europe. He made his famous statement that the United States must use Lend-Lease to become "the great arsenal of democracy" and supply the Allies with war materials.[11] He also told Congress on January 6, 1941, that American policy in the global crisis would be determined by the search for "four essential human freedoms."[12] These were the freedom of speech, freedom of worship, freedom from want, and freedom from fear.

Dictators continued their attacks in Europe and Asia. In June 1941, Hitler broke his nonaggression pact and invaded Russia. FDR asked Congress to extend Lend-Lease to the Russians. In July, the Japanese seized the capital of Vietnam. Because American intelligence had broken Japanese codes, the United States knew the Japanese next planned to conquer the Dutch East

Indies. They ignored FDR's warnings to stop their advances. Roosevelt then cut off all oil shipments to Japan. It was impossible to wage war without oil to fuel ships and airplanes. The Japanese planned possible takeovers of British and Dutch islands in the Pacific, which had rich caches of oil. At the same time, they negotiated with United States leaders about restoring positive relations.

In August 1941, FDR met British prime minister Winston Churchill for the first time. Aboard the *Augusta,* anchored off Newfoundland, Canada, they secretly planned the Atlantic Charter. It was a joint strategy, set in place in case the United States entered the war. The charter listed eight common principles on which to build a better future for the world. It also called for "the final destruction of the Nazi tyranny."[13] As the two leaders worked on the agreement, they formed a close bond.

In September 1941, a Nazi U-boat fired on the American destroyer U.S.S. *Greer.* The attack occurred at a tragic time in FDR's life. His mother died on September 7, 1941, of a blood clot in her lung. Her death delayed his public reaction to the *Greer* incident. FDR went to Hyde Park to sort through his mother's things. He found a box containing his baby toys and gifts he had made for his mother when he was young. Tears rolled down his face. It was the first time anyone on his staff had ever seen him cry.[14]

Eleanor Roosevelt comforted her husband during

Roosevelt and Prime Minister Winston Churchill of Great Britain met on the U.S.S. Augusta from August 9–12, 1941. They developed the Atlantic Charter. Roosevelt is grasping the arm of his son Elliott.

this rough time. However, she must have felt a sense of relief that her dominating mother-in-law was gone.[15] Perhaps now she and Franklin could arrange Springwood to be their home. Unfortunately for Eleanor, FDR wanted nothing changed.

World events commanded Roosevelt to return to work. On September 11, 1941, he gave a Fireside Chat to respond to the German attacks on American ships. He announced that United States vessels would now fire on German ships on sight.

In October, American intelligence learned that the Japanese government planned to attack, sometime after November 29, 1941. The exact date and location were not known. The messages worried Roosevelt. He said, ". . . we must all be prepared for real trouble, possibly soon."[16] Most United States officials thought the Japanese would attack British or Dutch islands in Southeast Asia or the South Pacific. A direct attack on United States forces seemed impossible. The major United States naval base at Pearl Harbor in Hawaii seemed safe, since it was thirty-four hundred miles away from Japan.

On the morning of Sunday, December 7, 1941, United States sailors at Pearl Harbor were sleeping or eating breakfast. At 7:55 A.M., Japanese planes dropped out of the sky, raining bombs on the harbor and nearby airfield. A soon-to-be famous radio message went out, "Air raid Pearl Harbor. This is no drill."[17] Half the United States Pacific fleet was anchored elsewhere. But the

SOURCE DOCUMENT

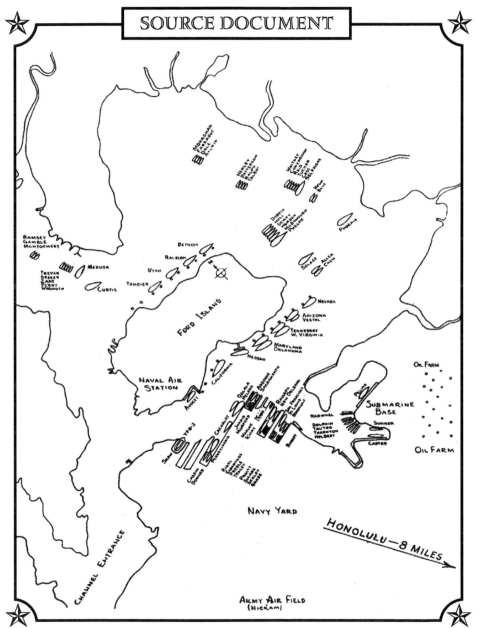

Chart of United States ship positions at the time of the Pearl Harbor attack on December 7, 1941.

ships in the harbor were anchored so close together that they made easy targets. Within minutes, all eight American battleships had been hit. Also hit were three destroyers, three light cruisers, four other ships, and 188 airplanes. In all, thirty-five hundred sailors, soldiers, and civilians died in this raid.

The day after the Pearl Harbor attack, Franklin D. Roosevelt went to the Capitol. He delivered a short but spellbinding speech to Congress. Nearly 60 million Americans listened to the speech on the radio. He called the attack "a date which will live in infamy."[18] He asked that Congress declare that "since the unprovoked and

The U.S.S. West Virginia *and the U.S.S.* Tennessee *after the attack by the Japanese on Pearl Harbor.*

dastardly attack by Japan on Sunday, December 7, 1941, a state of war has existed between the United States and the Japanese Empire."[19] With the exception of one vote, both houses of Congress approved the declaration of war. The time of waiting was over. Americans were optimistic they would win the war.

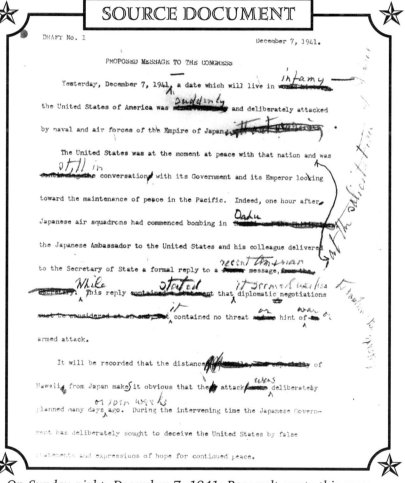

SOURCE DOCUMENT

DRAFT No. 1   December 7, 1941.

PROPOSED MESSAGE TO THE CONGRESS

Yesterday, December 7, 1941, a date which will live in *infamy*

the United States of America was *suddenly* and deliberately attacked

by naval and air forces of the Empire of Japan.

The United States was at the moment at peace with that nation and was *still in* conversation with its Government and its Emperor looking

toward the maintenance of peace in the Pacific. Indeed, one hour after,

Japanese air squadrons had commenced bombing in *Oahu*

the Japanese Ambassador to the United States and his colleague delivered

to the Secretary of State a formal reply to a *recent American* message.

While stated This reply contained *it seemed useless* that diplomatic negotiations

it contained no threat *or* hint of *war or* armed attack.

It will be recorded that the distance of

Hawaii from Japan makes it obvious that the attack *was* deliberately

or even weeks planned many days ago. During the intervening time the Japanese Govern-

ment has deliberately sought to deceive the United States by false

statements and expressions of hope for continued peace.

On Sunday night, December 7, 1941, Roosevelt wrote this message to give to Congress the following morning. Note how his handwritten corrections made the speech more powerful.

8

WAR, PEACE, AND DEATH

For the second time in twenty-five years, Americans were fighting a world war. On December 11, 1941, Germany and Italy declared war on the United States. Congress immediately declared war on these two nations, with no dissenting votes. Although the war would not be fought on American soil, the United States would never be the same. American industrial might would ensure the defeat of the Axis; and America, under FDR's leadership, would emerge a world leader.

FDR and British prime minister Churchill held lively meetings in Washington, beginning on December 22, 1941. Churchill stayed at the White House and mounted a map tracking the progress of the war next door to his bedroom. Churchill worried that the Pearl Harbor attack would cause the United States to focus on the war in the Pacific rather than the battlefields of Europe. FDR soon reassured him that Germany was the main enemy to be defeated first.[1]

Domestic problems still existed, but FDR directed most of his attention to winning the war. He called himself the Commander in Chief rather than the president. FDR showed optimism and determination, just as he had in fighting the Great Depression and his own illness.

Headlines of war dominate this extra edition of The Seattle Daily Times *on December 8, 1941.*

All four Roosevelt sons served in the United States military and returned home safely. James was a Marine. Elliott served in the Army Air Corps. FDR, Jr., and John were in the Navy.

The United States was unprepared for war. Its military forces in 1941 ranked nineteenth in the world, smaller than Belgium's. Ships, aircraft, and arms were scarce.

The war effort healed the economy in a way the New Deal could not. Unemployment virtually disappeared. Shipyards and many factories operated around the clock. By 1944, American businesses manufactured 44 percent of the entire world's military supplies. In some parts of the country, personal incomes rose 100 percent or more.[2] Industrial production rose 100 percent.[3]

FDR established the War Production Board (WPB) to assist the factory changeover from civilian to military production. The WPB determined which factories would receive scarce materials such as rubber and tin. The Office of Price Administration (OPA) set price limits and rationed scarce goods. Families were issued ration books, which were distributed at local schools. Coupons inside these books allowed people to purchase certain amounts of meats, coffee, sugar, canned goods, dairy products, and shoes.

FDR wanted to maintain public morale despite the need for war sacrifices. Professional baseball was allowed to continue. Although most steel went into making ships, FDR set aside enough for beer and soft drink bottle caps.

The war effort changed the very structure of American society. Women worked in shipyards, aircraft plants, and government offices. By the end of the war, over 36 percent of women held jobs.[4] By contrast, in 1940, women had made up only about 25 percent of the total labor force.[5]

More African Americans got better jobs. In 1941, FDR formed the Fair Employment Practices Commission, which forbade discrimination in government and defense industries. African Americans also served in the armed forces, but usually in separate units. By war's end, some integration had occurred.

Although FDR played a leadership role in fighting discrimination, he virtually ignored the mass slaughter of European Jews. As early as 1942, he had received evidence of secret Nazi death camps. By the end of the war, 6 million Jews and another 5 million people of various "undesirable" groups had been murdered in Nazi gas chambers. Both American and British leaders refused to bomb the death camps or the railroad lines leading to them. They insisted such actions would take bombers away from military missions. FDR felt that defeating Hitler was the only way to help the Jews.[6] He would not try to bribe Hitler or negotiate with him to release any prisoners. He insisted that Hitler be totally defeated, or surrender unconditionally.[7] Many Jews wished to establish a homeland in Palestine (now Israel), but the

Rosie the Riveter became a symbol of the war effort. Many women went to work during the war. They took the jobs previously held by men who were now overseas fighting.

situation in the Middle East was not stable enough at that time. Roosevelt felt that the war must be won first. Then political issues such as the creation of a new nation could be tackled.[8] In opinion polls of the time, the majority of Americans showed they were unwilling to allow increased Jewish immigration to the United States, even though they knew about Hitler's treatment of the Jews.[9]

Roosevelt's handling of Japanese Americans also received criticism. Government officials in California feared that the Japanese would next attack the West Coast. The attack on Pearl Harbor had stirred up hostility against Japanese people. Many Americans distrusted anyone of Japanese ancestry even though no Japanese Americans ever spied for Japan during World War II. FDR gave in to public pressure and on February 19, 1942, signed Executive Order 9066. It created the War Relocation Authority (WRA), which ordered more than ten thousand Japanese Americans to leave their homes and businesses. Two thirds of them were American citizens. They were sent to camps in isolated desert areas of the western United States until "their loyalty could be determined." Conditions were harsh and lacked privacy. The Japanese Americans remained in these relocation centers until nearly the end of the war. In 1988, many years after the war, Congress apologized and paid them reparations (damages awarded for wrongdoing). Despite their detestable treatment, many Japanese Americans served in the United States military.

From December 1941 to June 1942, the Allies lost many battles to the Japanese in the Pacific and to Hitler's forces in Russia. On Washington's birthday, 1942, FDR gave a Fireside Chat aimed at restoring the public's optimism. More than 61 million adults, almost 80 percent of the total possible radio audience, listened. FDR asked listeners to have a map in front of them as he traced his strategy. He compared the war to the early years of the American Revolutionary War when George Washington's Continental Army faced terrible odds and suffered many defeats.[10] He cautioned that Americans had to be prepared to suffer more losses "before the turn of the tide."[11]

The Allies had learned that the Germans were working to build an atomic bomb. In August 1942, FDR created the Manhattan Project, a top secret effort aimed at developing and perfecting an atomic weapon before the Germans did.

By the end of 1942, the Allies had won several battles. In the Pacific that summer, they defeated the Japanese Navy in the battles of the Coral Sea, Midway, and Guadalcanal.

In Europe, the United States was not fighting alone. That meant FDR had help in the battles, but less control over planning them. FDR decided to support the British plan to invade North Africa. He felt the Allies were not yet strong enough for a cross-channel invasion of

German-occupied France.[12] The German forces in North Africa surrendered in May 1943, after six months of tough fighting.

In January 1943, FDR became the first president to fly in an airplane during his term in office. He flew to meet Churchill in Casablanca, Morocco, to plan the Allied invasion of Sicily, off the coast of Italy.

In November 1943, Soviet leader Joseph Stalin met Roosevelt and Churchill in Teheran, Iran. "The Big Three" agreed on a cross-channel invasion to take place at Normandy, France. Stalin promised that once Germany was defeated, the Soviets would join the war against Japan. All three leaders agreed to support a new international peacekeeping body, the United Nations. After meeting in Teheran, FDR came down with influenza. He never completely recovered his health.

Late in 1943, FDR began to call himself "Dr. Win-the-War." He said "Dr. New Deal" no longer existed.[13] He believed the need to win the war was greater than the need for domestic reform. Thus, he was willing to accept defeat of New Deal measures in exchange for congressional support of the war.

FDR asked his daughter Anna to move into the White House with her children. Her second husband, John Boettiger, was overseas with the Army. Anna became a trusted advisor to her father. He was especially lonely because Eleanor traveled often.

In January 1944, FDR received evidence that his own State Department had prevented Jewish refugees from entering the United States.[14] Roosevelt created the War Refugee Board. Unfortunately, his action came too late to help thousands of Jews.

By March 1944, FDR was experiencing many physical problems. His doctor, Admiral Ross McIntire, was an ear, nose, and throat specialist who seemed unaware of the decline in Roosevelt's health. Finally, he sent FDR for a checkup at Bethesda Naval Hospital. Heart specialist Howard G. Bruenn found that FDR had suffered a heart attack and also had high blood pressure, heart disease, and acute bronchitis. Bruenn insisted that FDR limit his daily activity and his smoking and go on a low-fat diet. FDR followed his doctor's instructions and his health gradually improved.

The cross-channel invasion, known as D-day, finally occurred on June 6, 1944. The Allied forces landed on the coast of Normandy and surprised the Germans who had occupied France. After brutal fighting, Paris was freed on August 25. By mid-September, the Allies controlled most of France and Belgium. The Soviets moved west into central Europe and attacked Berlin.

From September 12–14, 1944, Churchill and Roosevelt met in Quebec, Canada. Churchill asked for a continuing Lend-Lease commitment. He was shocked by the decline in FDR's appearance. He was thin, his color was poor, and his hands shook.

Allied fortunes continued to improve in the Pacific. On October 20, General Douglas MacArthur landed in the Philippines. In the largest naval battle in history, the Battle of Leyte Gulf, the Japanese Navy was destroyed.

FDR debated whether or not to run for an unprecedented fourth term. He said, "All that is within me cries out to go back to my home on the Hudson River."[15] But if the people wanted him to continue as their wartime leader, he would. He told his son James, "The people elected me their leader and I can't quit in the middle of the war."[16]

Thomas E. Dewey, the governor of New York, was his Republican opponent in 1944. A key campaign issue was the president's health. In addition to his other problems, he was suffering from arteriosclerosis, or the thickening and hardening of the arteries. Arteries are the vessels that carry blood away from the heart. FDR had dark circles under his eyes and his hands shook.

But the excitement of campaigning injected him with new energy. He made several campaign appearances to show that his health was good. FDR won 53.5 percent of the popular vote compared to Dewey's 46 percent. Harry Truman was elected vice-president.

In keeping with a nation at war, the inauguration was a simple ceremony held on January 20, 1945. By this time, the Roosevelts had thirteen grandchildren. FDR wanted all of them at his inauguration.

Two days later, FDR left for Yalta in the Crimea. There, the Big Three—FDR, Churchill, and Stalin—reviewed the military situation and made postwar plans. FDR hoped to get Stalin's promise to form a

Roosevelt wanted all thirteen of his grandchildren present at his fourth inauguration ceremony on January 20, 1945. This was their last family portrait.

Polish government that represented all five major political parties of that nation. But Stalin did not want to give up control in Poland. He wanted Poland as a buffer between the Soviet Union and Germany. Only another world war would force him to give up the territory he had just won in World War II. However, he did promise to allow postwar elections in the conquered territory. The Big Three also agreed to hold an international meeting in April in San Francisco to form the United Nations peacekeeping body.

FDR was later criticized for giving in to Stalin, allowing him to keep the captured lands. Defenders and Roosevelt himself maintained that he had done the best he could at the time.[17] He needed Russia to help defeat Germany and Japan. Stalin's postwar actions showed that he had no intention of allowing elections. But FDR did not know then what we know now, that Stalin would go back on his promises. At the time, FDR could not risk starting another war.

Two days after he returned from Yalta, FDR addressed Congress. He entered the Capitol in a wheelchair, something he had never done before in public. A

The "Big Three" at Yalta: (left to right) British prime minister Winston Churchill, Roosevelt, Soviet leader Joseph Stalin. At Yalta on the Crimean Peninsula, February 4–12, 1945, the world leaders made plans for the defeat of Germany.

hush fell over the Senate chamber. Roosevelt's gray skin and trembling voice and hands shocked congressional leaders.

After the speech, FDR went to Warm Springs for a badly needed vacation. From there he planned to go to San Francisco on April 25 to open the United Nations conference.

On the morning of April 12, 1945, FDR told Dr. Bruenn that he had a slight headache.[18] He signed papers and worked on the speech he planned to give on Thomas Jefferson Day, April 14. At 1:15 P.M., FDR announced, "I have a terrific headache."[19] He slumped

After Yalta, Roosevelt spoke to Congress on March 1, 1945. His physical appearance had deteriorated badly.

over and never regained consciousness. FDR was dead of a cerebral hemorrhage, severe bleeding in the brain.

His death became a symbol for all American losses in battle. His name was printed on the war casualty lists for that day. For years, many Americans could remember exactly where they were and what they were doing the moment they heard about FDR's death. Broadcaster Edward R. Murrow reported from London that Churchill had tears in his eyes when he said, "One day the world, and history, will know what it owes your president."[20]

When FDR died, one of the guests staying at the Little White House was Lucy Mercer (now Lucy Mercer Rutherfurd, a wealthy widow). FDR had broken his promise to his wife and arranged several secret visits with Mrs. Rutherfurd. She was hustled away from Warm Springs before Eleanor Roosevelt arrived.

Eleanor Roosevelt flew down to escort her husband's body back to Washington, D.C. Mourners lined the route of the funeral train. In the capital, six white horses pulled the wagon holding the flag-draped coffin down Pennsylvania Avenue. After the funeral in the East Room of the White House, the coffin was taken by train to Hyde Park. There, FDR received a twenty-one gun salute. Fala, the pet Scottie, barked at each shot. The coffin was lowered into a grave in the rose garden where FDR had played as a child. In keeping with his wishes, the location was marked by a simple stone carved only with his name.

Vice-President Harry S. Truman was now the president. Two weeks later, on April 30, Hitler committed suicide. On May 7, Germany surrendered. An atomic bomb was dropped on Hiroshima, Japan, on August 6, 1945. Three days later, Nagasaki, Japan, was also bombed. The atomic weapons caused horrible destruction and convinced the Japanese to surrender.

Debate continues today over President Truman's use of the atomic bomb. Although it was under development when he was vice-president, Truman did not find out about the bomb until after FDR's death. Some historians felt Truman viewed the bomb solely as a military weapon, a quick way to end the war.[21] Others felt he also meant its use as a way to demonstrate United States might to Russian leaders. In his lifetime, FDR had been concerned about the morality of using the bomb as a weapon and about the postwar use of its power. But he had not discussed his concerns with Truman.

Although FDR did not live to see the official end of the war, Eleanor carried out her husband's dream of involvement in the United Nations. She was one of the delegates at the first general assembly of the United Nations on January 10, 1946.

9

LEGACY

Franklin Delano Roosevelt became president during the Great Depression, one of the worst economic times in United States history. At his death, the nation was a superpower. When nominated for the presidency, FDR promised a New Deal for the American people, who were fearful and discouraged. British philosopher Isaiah Berlin wrote that Roosevelt was one of the few leaders in history "who seemed to have no fear of the future."[1] FDR filled his speeches and Fireside Chats with optimism and enthusiasm.

Almost daily during the beginning of his presidency, he proposed new legislation to wage war against the Great Depression. Many of these measures still exist today, such as Social Security, the minimum wage, maximum working hours, and unemployment insurance.

However, not all Americans supported Roosevelt's actions. Many members of his own wealthy social class refused to call him by name. They felt he was moving the country toward socialism, where the federal government exercises great power over citizens' lives. Some Americans today still feel that FDR created a welfare state with too many government assistance programs. However, FDR believed strongly in the duty of a democracy to guard the welfare of all its citizens. In addition, he had a continuing interest in the needs of his fellow human beings. His life was built on a Christian faith that led him to want to help others, especially those less fortunate.

During Roosevelt's second term in office, dictators began to exert control in many nations of the world. The United States had traditionally followed a policy of isolationism, or keeping itself outside of, or isolated from, other countries' affairs. When World War II broke out, Americans did not want to be involved. FDR respected the voters' wishes, although he sensed America would eventually be drawn into war. After the bombing of Pearl Harbor, FDR became an enthusiastic Commander in Chief. Using his widely broadcast Fireside Chats, he rallied Americans around the war effort. Through increased war production, he restored the economy, something the New Deal measures had failed to accomplish. FDR looked forward to establishing a peacekeeping body after the war. Although he did not live to see its formation, the United Nations continues today.

FDR believed in democratic ideals, such as the right of nations to choose their own governments. But, in fact, he delayed helping the Jews and allowed Japanese Americans to be imprisoned in the United States. If he did not want to hear what a visitor had to say, he would monopolize the conversation. He promised his wife he would not see his mistress, Lucy Mercer Rutherfurd, again, yet he resumed this relationship in the 1940s.

Roosevelt, however, was willing to try new programs and had an unquenchable curiosity about many subjects. He loved serving as president and had an uncanny ability to read public opinion. He sensed when to use the power of his office and when to pull back. "I am like a cat," he said. "I make a quick stroke and then I relax."[2] Despite his privileged upbringing, he was a practical, down-to-earth individual. Winston Churchill once compared his bubbly personality to opening a bottle of champagne.[3]

Controversy exists over the effect his polio had on FDR. Frances Perkins, his secretary of labor, wrote that FDR "underwent a spiritual transformation during the years of his illness" and dropped his slightly arrogant attitude.[4] He became aware of other people and their needs. Eleanor Roosevelt felt the disease was a turning point for her husband and that it gave him strength and courage he had not had before.[5]

However, his son James felt his father already had a strong character. James said, "I believe it was not polio that forged Father's character but that it was Father's character that enabled him to rise above his affliction."[6] Polio could not have caused him to develop traits such as determination, patience, and depth. James Roosevelt felt his father would have reached the presidency anyway. The polio attack had simply delayed FDR's progress. His illness also won FDR sympathy from the general public.[7]

Each person must draw his or her own conclusions about FDR and the reasons for his actions. He did not write an autobiography. Our opinions must be based on Roosevelt's speeches, letters, and what others have written about him.

FDR showed an ongoing interest in the treatment of polio. On September 23, 1937, he created the National Foundation for Infantile Paralysis. The goal of the foundation was to raise money for the treatment of polio and to research its causes. Through its fund drive, the March of Dimes, millions of dollars have been raised.

FDR willed his house at Hyde Park and its furnishings to the American public. Both Eleanor and Franklin Roosevelt are buried in the rose garden. Next door, on the same grounds, is the Franklin D. Roosevelt Library and Museum, the nation's first presidential library.

The FDR Memorial opened in Washington, D.C., on May 2, 1997. Its granite walls are arranged in four open-sided, roofless rooms, one per term of FDR's presidency. Quotations from his speeches have been sandblasted into the walls. The handicapped can move easily from room to room. Tall pillars are embossed in

Braille, so the blind can experience the memorial directly. Designer Lawrence Halprin wanted to pay tribute to FDR's ability to "face challenges and create solutions." However, controversy arose from some handicapped-rights supporters. They wanted FDR to be shown seated in a wheelchair instead of an easy chair. Curtis Roosevelt, one of FDR's grandsons, maintained that FDR would not have wished to be shown in the wheelchair.[8] The completed monument displays a nine-foot-tall sculpture of FDR seated in a chair. A cape is draped over his shoulders and Fala sits at his feet.

This is room three of the FDR memorial where a nine-foot sculpture shows Roosevelt in his treasured naval cape. His beloved dog, Fala, is at his feet. The quotation on the wall is from Roosevelt's address given at the annual dinner of the White House Correspondents' Association on March 15, 1941.

FDR forever changed the shape of American society. Women and African Americans entered the workforce in increasing numbers and in new types of jobs. The government assumed more control over the lives of its citizens with programs such as unemployment insurance, Social Security, and stock market and banking regulation. The United States changed from an isolationist nation to a superpower with a strong military force.

FDR loved being president. Historian Eric Larrabee wrote of him:

> More than any other man, he ran the war, and ran it well enough to deserve the gratitude of his countrymen then and since, and of those from whom he lifted the yoke of the Axis tyrannies. His conduct as Commander in Chief . . . bears the mark of greatness.[9]

Chronology

1882—Born at Springwood, Hyde Park, New York, on January 30.

1896—Attends Groton School in Massachusetts.
–1900

1900—Enters Harvard University in Cambridge, Massachusetts.

1903—Graduates from Harvard University, June 24.

1904—Enters Columbia Law School.

1905—Marries distant cousin Anna Eleanor Roosevelt on March 17.

1906—Birth of daughter Anna, May 3.

1907—Birth of son James, December 23.

1909—Birth of first Franklin D. Roosevelt, Jr., March 18; death of Franklin D. Roosevelt, Jr., November 9.

1910—Birth of son Elliott, September 23.

1910—Serves as New York state senator.
–1913

1913—Serves as assistant secretary of the Navy.
–1919

1914—World War I begins, August 4; birth of second Franklin D. Roosevelt, Jr., August 17.

1916—Birth of son John, March 13.

1917—United States Congress declares war on Germany, April 6.

1920—Nominated as Democratic vice-presidential candidate.

1921—Stricken with polio.

1928—Elected governor of New York.

1929—Stock market crashes, October 29.

1930—Reelected governor of New York.

1932—Elected president of the United States.

1936—Elected for second term as president.

1939—Germany invades Poland, and World War II begins.

1940—Elected for third term as president; trades Great Britain destroyers for bases.

1941—Lend-Lease plan supplies aid to Great Britain; announces Atlantic Charter with British prime minister Winston Churchill; Japanese attack Pearl Harbor, Hawaii, December 7; United States declares war on Japan and enters World War II, December 8.

1944—Elected for fourth term as president.

1945—Attends Yalta Conference with Winston Churchill and Soviet leader Joseph Stalin in February; dies at the age of sixty-three in Warm Springs, Georgia, at the Little White House, April 12.

Chapter Notes

Chapter 1. Trial by Fire

1. Kenneth S. Davis, *FDR: The Beckoning of Destiny, 1882–1928* (New York: Random House, 1972), p. 648.

2. Frank Freidel, *Franklin D. Roosevelt: A Rendezvous With Destiny* (Boston: Little, Brown and Company, 1990), p. 41.

3. Hugh Gregory Gallagher, *FDR's Splendid Deception* (Arlington, Va.: Vandamere Press, 1994), p. 9.

4. Joseph P. Lash, *Eleanor and Franklin* (New York: W. W. Norton & Company, Inc., 1971), p. 267.

5. Davis, p. 671.

6. Thomas Parrish, *Roosevelt and Marshall* (New York: William Morrow and Company, Inc., 1989), p. 29.

Chapter 2. A Privileged Birth

1. Geoffrey C. Ward, *Before the Trumpet: Young Franklin Roosevelt, 1882–1905* (New York: Harper & Row, 1985), p. 61.

2. Ibid., p. 110.

3. Kenneth S. Davis, *FDR: The Beckoning of Destiny, 1882–1928* (New York: Random House, 1972), p. 63.

4. Ward, p. 121.

5. Davis, p. 67.

6. Ward, p. 151.

7. Ibid.

8. Joseph P. Lash, *Eleanor and Franklin* (New York: W. W. Norton & Company, Inc., 1971), p. 116.

9. Ward, pp. 128–129.

10. Davis, p. 69.

11. Ward, pp. 139–140.

12. Davis, p. 71.

13. Ward, p. 163.

14. Ibid., p. 173.

15. Ibid., p. 180.

16. James MacGregor Burns, *Roosevelt: The Lion and the Fox* (San Diego, Calif.: Harcourt Brace & Company, 1956), p. 11.

17. Ward, pp. 193–194.

18. Ibid., p. 181.

19. Davis, p. 128.

20. Burns, p. 15.

21. Ward, p. 236.

22. Lash, p. 120.

23. Burns, p. 18.

24. Davis, p. 140.

Chapter 3. Anna Eleanor

1. Kenneth S. Davis, *FDR: The Beckoning of Destiny, 1882–1928* (New York: Random House, 1972), p. 177.

2. Joseph P. Lash, *Eleanor and Franklin* (New York: W. W. Norton & Company, Inc., 1971), p. 87.

3. Ibid., p. 102.

4. Ibid., p. 141.

5. Rexford G. Tugwell, *FDR: Architect of an Era* (New York: The Macmillan Company, 1967), pp. 34–35.

6. Davis, p. 204.

7. Lash, p. 162.

8. Ibid.

9. Elliott Roosevelt and James Brough, *An Untold Story: The Roosevelts of Hyde Park* (New York: G. P. Putnam's Sons, 1973), p. 48.

10. Ibid.

11. Lash, p. 167.

Chapter 4. A Messy Business

1. Joseph P. Lash, *Eleanor and Franklin* (New York: W. W. Norton & Company, Inc., 1971), p. 167.

2. James MacGregor Burns, *Roosevelt: The Lion and the Fox* (San Diego, Calif.: Harcourt Brace & Company, 1956), p. 33.

3. The Seventeenth Amendment to the Constitution was ratified in 1913. It changed the selection of United States senators to direct election by the voters of each state. The amendment stated, in part, that "The Senate of the United States shall be composed of two Senators from each State, elected by the people thereof, for six years; and each Senator shall have one vote."

4. Kenneth S. Davis, *FDR: The Beckoning of Destiny, 1882–1928* (New York: Random House, 1972), p. 292.

5. Elliott Roosevelt and James Brough, *An Untold Story: The Roosevelts of Hyde Park* (New York: G. P. Putnam's Sons, 1973), p. 19.

6. Eric Foner and John A. Garraty, eds., *The Reader's Companion to American History* (Boston: Houghton Mifflin Company, 1991), p. 1171.

7. Woodrow Wilson, "Speech for Declaration of War Against Germany," in Richard Hofstadter and Beatrice K. Hofstadter, eds., *Great Issues in American History: From Reconstruction to the Present Day, 1864–1981* (New York: Vintage Books, 1982), p. 208.

8. Thomas Parrish, *Roosevelt and Marshall* (New York: William Morrow and Company, Inc., 1989), p. 27.

9. Frank Freidel, *Franklin D. Roosevelt: A Rendezvous With Destiny* (Boston: Little, Brown and Company, 1990), pp. 30–31.

10. Lash, p. 220.

11. Ibid., p. 226.

12. Freidel, pp. 32–33.

13. Vincent Wilson, Jr., *The Book of the Presidents* (Brookeville, Md.: American History Research Associates, 1993), p. 62.

14. Rexford G. Tugwell, *FDR: Architect of an Era* (New York: The Macmillan Company, 1967), p. 56.

Chapter 5. A Challenging Time

1. James MacGregor Burns, *Roosevelt: The Lion and the Fox* (San Diego, Calif.: Harcourt Brace & Company, 1956), p. 76.

2. Hugh Gregory Gallagher, *FDR's Splendid Deception* (Arlington, Va.: Vandamere Press, 1994), p. 18.

3. Thomas Parrish, *Roosevelt and Marshall* (New York: William Morrow and Company, Inc., 1989), p. 29.

4. Gallagher, p. 19.

5. Joseph P. Lash, *Eleanor and Franklin* (New York: W. W. Norton & Company, Inc., 1971), p. 273.

6. Burns, p. 90.

7. Frank Freidel, *Franklin D. Roosevelt: A Rendezvous With Destiny* (Boston: Little, Brown and Company, 1990), p. 42.

8. Gallagher, p. 22.

9. Ibid.

10. Ibid.

11. Kenneth S. Davis, *FDR: The Beckoning of Destiny 1882–1928* (New York: Random House, 1972), pp. 635–656.

12. Ibid., p. 677.

13. Gallagher, p. 60.

14. Burns, p. 93.

15. Davis, p. 756.

16. Burns, p. 99.

17. Ibid., p. 101.

18. Gallagher, p. 73.

19. Frances Perkins, *The Roosevelt I Knew* (New York: Viking Press, 1946), p. 44.

20. Freidel, p. 65.

21. Ibid.

22. Ibid., p. 73.

Chapter 6. The New Deal

1. James MacGregor Burns, *Roosevelt: The Lion and the Fox* (San Diego, Calif.: Harcourt Brace & Company, 1956), p. 133.

2. The 20th Amendment to the Constitution changed the inauguration to January beginning with the 1936 election.

3. Joy Hakim, *War, Peace, and All That Jazz* (New York: Oxford University Press, 1995), p. 101.

4. Franklin D. Roosevelt, *FDR Speaks: The FDR Memorial Collection*, Room One Pamphlet, Parks & History Association, Washington, D.C., 1997, p. 3.

5. Ibid., p. 5.

6. Joseph P. Lash, *Eleanor and Franklin* (New York: W. W. Norton & Company, Inc., 1971), p. 355.

7. Joseph P. Lash, *Love, Eleanor* (New York: Doubleday & Company, Inc., 1982), p. 130.

8. Lash, *Eleanor and Franklin*, p. 357.

9. James MacGregor Burns, *Roosevelt: The Soldier of Freedom* (San Diego, Calif.: Harcourt Brace Jovanovich, Publishers, 1970), p. 58.

10. Peter Collier, *The Roosevelts: An American Saga* (New York: Simon & Schuster, 1994), p. 347.

11. Burns, *Lion*, p. 168.

12. Ibid., p. 176.

13. Doris Kearns Goodwin, *No Ordinary Time* (New York: Simon & Schuster, 1994), p. 57.

14. Collier, p. 351.

15. Anne O'Hare McCormick, "Vast Tides that Stir the Capital," in Frank Freidel, *The New Deal and the American People* (Englewood Cliffs, N.J.: Prentice-Hall, Inc., 1965), pp. 6–7.

16. Eric Foner and John A. Garraty, eds., *The Reader's Companion to American History* (Boston: Houghton Mifflin Company, 1991), p. 177.

17. Thomas Parrish, *Roosevelt and Marshall* (New York: William Morrow and Company, Inc., 1989), p. 57.

18. Alan Brinkley, *American History: A Survey* (New York: McGraw-Hill, Inc., 1995), p. 681.

19. Freidel, p. 136.

20. Brinkley, p. 708.

21. Rexford G. Tugwell, *FDR: Architect of an Era* (New York: The Macmillan Company, 1967), p. 138.

22. Marquis Childs, "They Hate Roosevelt," in Frank Freidel, *The New Deal*, pp. 99, 103.

23. Franklin D. Roosevelt, *FDR Speaks: The FDR Memorial Collection,* Eagle Alcove Pamphlet, Parks & History Association, Washington, D.C., 1997, p. 4.

24. Ibid., p. 10.

25. Franklin D. Roosevelt, *FDR Speaks: The FDR Memorial Collection,* Room Two Pamphlet, Parks & History Association, Washington, D.C., 1997, p. 7.

26. Ibid., p. 8.

27. Franklin D. Roosevelt, "Radio Address on Supreme Court Reform," in Richard Hofstadter and Beatrice K. Hofstadter, eds. *Great Issues in American History: From Reconstruction to the Present Day, 1864–1981* (New York: Vintage Books, 1982), p. 366.

Chapter 7. Threats of War

1. Alan Brinkley, *American History: A Survey* (New York: McGraw-Hill, Inc., 1995), p. 735.

2. Franklin D. Roosevelt, "Quarantine the Aggressors Speech," in Richard Hofstadter and Beatrice K. Hofstadter, eds., *Great Issues in American History: From Reconstruction to the Present Day, 1864–1981* (New York: Vintage Books, 1982), p. 379.

3. Frank Freidel, *Franklin D. Roosevelt: A Rendezvous With Destiny* (Boston: Little, Brown and Company, 1990), p. 264.

4. Brinkley, p. 736.

5. Thomas Parrish, *Roosevelt and Marshall* (New York: William Morrow and Company, Inc., 1989), p. 101.

6. Freidel, p. 322.

7. Brinkley, p. 738.

8. Ibid., p. 739.

9. Burton K. Wheeler, "Speech on Lend-Lease," in Hofstadter, p. 392.

10. James MacGregor Burns, *Roosevelt: The Soldier of Freedom* (San Diego, Calif.: Harcourt Brace Jovanovich, Publishers, 1970), p. 48.

11. Franklin D. Roosevelt, *FDR Speaks: The FDR Memorial Collection,* Passageway Pamphlet, Parks & History Association, Washington, D.C., p. 12.

12. Franklin D. Roosevelt, *FDR Speaks: The FDR Memorial Collection,* Room Four Pamphlet, Parks & History Association, Washington, D.C., p. 15.

13. "The Atlantic Charter," in Hofstadter, p. 400.

14. Doris Kearns Goodwin, *No Ordinary Time* (New York: Simon & Schuster, 1994), p. 274.

15. Joseph P. Lash, *Eleanor and Franklin* (New York: W. W. Norton & Company, Inc., 1971), p. 643.

16. Freidel, p. 399.

17. Parrish, p. 208.

18. Roosevelt, "War Message to Congress," in Hofstadter, p. 401.

19. Ibid., pp. 402–403.

Chapter 8. War, Peace, and Death

1. James MacGregor Burns, *Roosevelt: The Soldier of Freedom* (San Diego, Calif.: Harcourt Brace Jovanovich, Publishers, 1970), p. 179.

2. Alan Brinkley, *American History: A Survey* (New York: McGraw-Hill-Inc., 1995), p. 751.

3. Doris Kearns Goodwin, *No Ordinary Time* (New York: Simon & Schuster, 1994), pp. 624–625.

4. Burns, p. 461.

5. Brinkley, p. 755.

6. Goodwin, pp. 454, 610.

7. Burns, p. 397.

8. Ibid., p. 545–546.

9. Goodwin, p. 102.

10. Ibid., p. 319.

11. Ibid., p. 320.

12. Ibid., p. 404.

13. Brinkley, p. 758.

14. Burns, p. 441.

15. Ibid., p. 612.

16. Hugh Gregory Gallagher, *FDR's Splendid Deception* (Arlington, Va.: Vandamere Press, 1994), p. 193.

17. Goodwin, p. 582.

18. Frank Freidel, *Franklin D. Roosevelt: A Rendezvous With Destiny* (Boston: Little, Brown, and Company, 1990), p. 605.

19. Ibid.

20. Ibid., p. 607.

21. Brinkley, p. 764.

Chapter 9. Legacy

1. Doris Kearns Goodwin, *No Ordinary Time* (New York: Simon & Schuster, 1994), p. 607.

2. Ibid., p. 608.

3. Ibid., p. 606.

4. Frances Perkins, *The Roosevelt I Knew* (New York: Viking Press, 1946), pp. 29–30.

5. Eleanor Roosevelt, *This I Remember* (New York: Harper & Brothers, 1949), p. 25.

6. Kenneth S. Davis, *FDR: The Beckoning of Destiny, 1882–1928* (New York: Random House, 1972), p. 678.

7. Ibid., p. 679.

8. Andrea Gabor, "Even Our Most Loved Monuments Had a Trial by Fire," *Smithsonian*, volume 28, no. 2, p. 106.

9. Goodwin, pp. 610–611.

Further Reading

Brown, Gene. *Conflict in Europe and the Great Depression: World War I (1914–1940)*. New York: Twenty-first Century Books, 1995.

Farrell, Jacqueline. *The Great Depression* (World History Series). San Diego, Calif.: Lucent Books, 1995.

Fremon, David K. *The Great Depression in American History.* Springfield, N.J.: Enslow Publishers, Inc., 1997.

Hacker, Jeffrey H. *Franklin D. Roosevelt.* Danbury, Conn.: Franklin Watts, Inc., 1983.

Larsen, Rebecca. *Franklin D. Roosevelt: Man of Destiny.* Danbury, Conn.: Franklin Watts, Inc., 1991.

Lawson, Don. *FDR's New Deal.* New York: HarperCollins Children's Books, 1979.

Nardo, Don. *Franklin D. Roosevelt: U.S. President (Great Achievers: Lives of the Physically Challenged).* New York: Chelsea House Publishers, 1995.

Roosevelt, Eleanor. *The Autobiography of Eleanor Roosevelt.* New York: HarperCollins Publishers, Inc., 1961.

Sandak, Cass R. *The Franklin Roosevelts.* Parsippany, N.J.: Silver Burdett Press, 1992.

Schuman, Michael A. *Franklin D. Roosevelt: The Four-Term President.* Springfield, N.J.: Enslow Publishers, Inc., 1996.

———. *Harry S. Truman.* Springfield, N.J.: Enslow Publishers, Inc., 1997.

Stewart, Gail B. *The New Deal.* New York: New Discovery Books, 1993.

Whitman, Sylvia. *V is for Victory: The American Home Front During World War II.* Minneapolis, Minn.: Lerner Publications Company, 1992.

Places to Visit

Campobello Island, New Brunswick, Canada

Roosevelt Campobello International Park. Phone: (506) 752-2922. Located across the bay from Lubec, Maine, the park includes the thirty-four room cottage FDR vacationed in. The visitor center shows a film about the Roosevelt family. Park open daily year-round. House open Memorial Day weekend to mid-October.

Hyde Park, New York

Home of Franklin D. Roosevelt National Historic Site. Phone: (914) 229-9115 or 229-2501. This house, where FDR grew up, has been left almost exactly as it was at his death. Displays include his childhood bird collection, leg braces, and wheelchair. Franklin and Eleanor Roosevelt are buried in the rose garden. Open daily, except January 1, Thanksgiving, and December 25.

Franklin D. Roosevelt Library and Museum. Phone: (914) 229-8114. E mail: library@roosevelt.nara.gov. The museum is on the same grounds as FDR's home. It has exhibits on the lives of both Franklin and Eleanor Roosevelt. Open the same as above.

Warm Springs, Georgia

Little White House State Historic Site. Phone: (706) 655-5870. This is the small cottage FDR built for his own retreat. It has been left the way it was on the day he died. A twelve-minute film on his life is shown. Open daily, except January 1, Thanksgiving, and December 25.

Washington, D.C.

Franklin Delano Roosevelt Memorial. Phone: (202) 619-7222 or (202) 426-6841. The memorial covers seven-and-a-half acres in West Potomac Park. It is arranged in four open-air rooms. Each room represents one of FDR's four presidential terms. Open daily.

Internet Addresses

The American Experience: The Presidents
    <http://www.pbs.org/wgbh/pages/amex/presidents/
        nf/featured/featured.html>

FDR Cartoon Archive
    <http://wizvax.net/nisk_hs/departments/social/
        fdr_html/FDRmain.hml>

FDR Memorial
    <http://www.nps.gov/fdrm/index2.html>

Franklin D. Roosevelt Library and Museum
    <http://www.academic.marist.edu/fdr/fdrintro.htm>

**The History Channel—Great Speeches: Hear the Words
That Changed the World**
    <http://www.historychannel.com/gspeech/archive. html>

**Inaugural Addresses of the Presidents
of the United States**
    <http://www.columbia.edu/acis/bartleby/inaugural/
        index.html>

**The Little White House State Historic
Site in Georgia**
    <http://www.gastateparks.org>

The Roosevelt Campobello International Park
    <http://www.nps.gov/roca>

The White House—Anna Eleanor Roosevelt
    <http://www.whitehouse.gov/WH/glimpse/firstladies/
        htmlar32.html>

The White House—Franklin D. Roosevelt
    <http://www.whitehouse.gov/WH/glimpse/presidents/html/
        fr32.html>

Index